Tennessee
Studies
In Literature

Editor
Allison R. Ensor

Associate Editor
Thomas J. A. Heffernan

VOLUME XXIII

THE UNIVERSITY OF TENNESSEE PRESS • KNOXVILLE • 1978

Tennessee Studies In Literature

EDITOR
Allison R. Ensor

ASSOCIATE EDITOR
Thomas J. A. Heffernan

EDITORIAL ASSISTANTS
Clyde W. Grotophorst
Cecilia Jane Quinn

Persons interested in submitting manuscripts should address the Editor, *Tennessee Studies In Literature,* Department of English, The University of Tennessee, Knoxville, Tennessee 37916. Contributions from any qualified scholar will be considered. Return postage should accompany manuscripts. Papers (ribbon copies on non-erasable bond paper) should be no longer than five thousand words. Other inquiries concerning this series should be addressed to The University of Tennessee Press, 293 Communications Building, University of Tennessee, Knoxville, Tennessee 37916.

This issue of
Tennessee Studies in Literature
is dedicated
to the memory of

ALWIN THALER
1891–1977

Professor of English Emeritus
A founding editor of this journal

CONTENTS

MARC D. GLASSER

MARRIAGE AND THE *SECOND NUN'S TALE*

Chaucer's many references to saints or their legends demonstrate the large part saints played in the conversation of common folk as well as his own easy familiarity with saints' lives and lore. John, the gullible carpenter of the *Miller's Tale*, and Harry Bailly are perhaps the Chaucerian characters who swear oaths in the names of saints most readily (and often humorously), but several of Chaucer's other characters can appeal to an appropriate saint on the spur of the moment.[1] Chauntecleer summarizes the life of Saint Kenelm in order to encourage Pertelote to believe in the premonitory power of dreams (B² 4300–11);[2] the Wife of Bath cites saints' lives as the only possible exception to the antifeminist writings of clerks (D 688–91); Criseyde anachronistically refers to saints' lives as the proper reading material for widows (*Troilus,* II 117–118); and the *Retraction* suggests in a list of tantalizing titles that Chaucer had written a number of "legendes of seintes" (I 1088), only one of which is extant. Despite the influence of classical biography, hagiography was one of the few original literary genres of the Christian Middle Ages,[3] and the fourteenth century was the age in which saints' legends began to be translated, copied, and circulated in compendious vernacular legendaries. It is, therefore, hardly surprising that a fourteenth-century Christian poet would allude to saints appropriately or that he would display an interest in hagiographical literature.[4]

Two reasonable questions to ask, then, in light of Chaucer's demonstrated interest in saints' legends, are: What is it about the Cecilia legend that attracted him, and why did he choose to include this one fully developed hagiographic legend in the *Canterbury Tales*? Although questions of authorial intent are difficult to answer definitively, two avenues are open to determine what drew Chaucer to the

1

legend of Saint Cecilia: one approach is to discover what, if anything, makes the Cecilia legend different from most other saints' lives; the other is to determine what relationship the *Second Nun's Tale*— Chaucer's version of the legend—has to the other Canterbury tales.

Because she was venerated as one of the early Christian martyrs, Cecilia's legend had been written numerous times before Chaucer undertook his "translacioun."[5] Cecilia's acts probably date from the early third century and became a part of theological and literary tradition no later than a century after her death. The fourth-century *Martyrologium Vetustissimum,* which is attributed to Jerome, contains references to Cecilia, her husband Valerian, and her brother-in-law Tiburce; other early martyrologies also preserve the important details of the legend, and such writers as Venantius Fortunatus, Bede, Aldhelm, Rabanus Maurus, Odo, Usuard, Simeon Metaphrastes, Surius, Alfred, Ælfric, Mombritius, and Jacobus of Voragine either wrote a Cecilia legend or show knowledge of her acts. By the fourteenth century vernacular versions of the legend circulated in several languages including Middle English.

The tradition and durability of Cecilia's fame account for Chaucer's knowledge of and access to her story, but why would he choose this legend as opposed to those of other equally well-known saints? At first glance the legend appears very similar to many other saints' lives. The story of the beautiful, high-born maiden, concerned about protecting her maidenhood and preserving her Christian faith, who is martyred for refusing to worship idols, is the standard fare in legends celebrating women saints. Agatha, Agnes, Katherine, Lucy, Margaret —this list could be expanded tenfold—all led lives quite like Cecilia's.[6] Their acts date from the early Christian era, and their legends are contained, like Cecilia's, in the immensely popular *Legenda Aurea,* Chaucer's major source for the *Second Nun's Tale,*[7] and in numerous Middle English translations.[8]

Each of these saints is a fair maiden whose major preoccupation is maintaining her virginity in order to serve Jesus. Each saint is wrenched from the cloistered life and forced to act in the violent world of persecutions and tortures. Each is pressured to renounce Christianity and worship the heathen gods, but each refuses and chooses instead a garish and spectacular martyrdom as a sign of her commitment to the faith. Like Cecilia, the other virgin martyrs denounce their pagan persecutors and miraculously triumph over their adversaries even as they submit to martyrdom. Margaret is bound and cast into a vessel filled with boiling water, but her bonds are miraculously broken, and she escapes unharmed. Agatha, Agnes, and Lucy also escape burning; Katherine is providentially freed from a torture wheel of knives. But all these saints, like Cecilia, are ultimately decapitated.

The numerous similarities between Cecilia's legend and those of the other virgins, however, can blur the significantly different features of her life. It is Cecilia's marriage which distinguishes her legend from those of the other virgin martyrs. Agatha, Agnes, Katherine, Lucy, and Margaret all have marriage offers forced upon them by their persecutors; invariably the offers are coupled with the condition that the saints renounce their faith; just as invariably the saints choose martyrdom rather than accept the marriage proposals.[9] Cecilia, however, marries her pagan suitor.[10]

As a result, Cecilia's marriage creates a structural framework which distinguishes her legend from those of the other virgin martyrs. Because she marries, she progresses through three stages in her development as a saint: from cautious maiden to married woman and finally to widow and zealous martyr. The framework encourages the reader to observe and contrast Cecilia's behavior in each of these three stages. In the course of her development, she encounters a problem which none of the other virgins face: after wedding Valerian she must convince him to share her faith as well as her commitment to the chaste life. She solves this problem on her wedding night, and it is this section of the legend which is pivotal to her growth as a saint.

The description of Cecilia and Valerian in bed on their marriage night humanizes and feminizes her in greater depth than the other virgins.[11] The marriage night enriches her character with pious love and concern for Valerian which contrasts with the fiery hatred she later displays toward the tyrant and persecutor Almachius. The marriage-night scene, in which she awakes to her calling as a proselytizer, delicately fuses Cecilia's public and personal motivations, her devotion to Christianity, and her love for her spouse. In contrast, then, to the other legends of virgin martyrs which Chaucer probably knew and might have chosen to translate, Cecilia's legend contains a structural pattern which organizes her progression toward sainthood and a plot sequence which illuminates her character more fully than that of Agnes, Agatha, Katherine, Lucy, or Margaret.

Of all the virgin-martyr legends available to Chaucer, he chose the life of Saint Cecilia, which has as its distinguishing feature the saint's marriage. Since marriage is an important concern throughout the *Canterbury Tales,* it should prove valuable to look carefully at how the marriage functions in the *Second Nun's Tale* and how the treatment of marriage there relates to the marriage theme elsewhere in the *Canterbury Tales.*

The body of criticism which elucidates the idea of marriage in the *Canterbury Tales* has grown large since Kittredge's famous article.[12] Some Chaucerians agree with the major premises of Kittredge's essay; others, though fewer in number, deny the existence of a Marriage Group; still others accept marriage as an important idea in Kittredge's Group but wish to include additional tales.[13] As long as dramatic interaction among the pilgrims is considered the *sine qua non* of the Marriage Group, the *Second Nun's Tale* will inevitably remain outside the dramatic boundaries of the Group. However, several critics have written about the marriage in the *Second Nun's Tale* and its relationship to other conjugal relationships in the *Canterbury Tales,* and there is general agreement about the usefulness and productiveness of Cecilia's marriage to Valerian. One writer, Donald Howard, has even suggested that the Cecilia-Valerian relationship is what the medieval Church might have called the "highest ideal." The title of Howard's article, "The Conclusion of the Marriage Group: Chaucer and the Human Condition,"[14] seems to assert that the *Second Nun's Tale* may have been Chaucer's final word on marriage in the *Canterbury Tales.* Howard's view of Cecilia's marriage, which has been supported by Joseph E. Grennen and Paul M. Clogan, is attractive in many respects.[15] Her marriage is the important initial motivation in Cecilia's progress toward sainthood, and I agree with the basic praise Howard, Grennen, and Clogan have for the Cecilia-Valerian relationship, but I shall argue that the marriage is neither an ideal nor a perfect one and that it is not a solution to the marriage question in the *Canterbury Tales.* The tale begins with the wedding and marriage night, and the marriage itself is short-lived. It is quickly overwhelmed by the "leveful bisynesse" of conversions and martyrdom. Marriage is presented as an important good in the *Second Nun's Tale,* but it is only the first step toward a greater good, that of heroic martyrdom.

The first stanza of the *Second Nun's Prologue* announces her purpose in telling the tale:

> That is to seyn, by leveful bisynesse,
> Wel oghten we to doon al oure entente,
> Lest that the feend thurgh ydelnesse us hente.   (G 5-7)

And three examples of "leveful bisynesse" are described in the remainder of the prologue. First the Nun prays to the Virgin Mary for aid in beginning her own "bisynesse," the translation of the legend. She next describes the prototypical act of feminine "bisynesse" in a beautiful "Invocacio ad Mariam" in which she plays poetically with the paradoxes inherent in Mary's act of creation (maid and mother; humble and high). In the "Interpretacio nominis Cecilie" the word *Cecilia* is said to mean, among other things, the "wey to the blynde" and the "hevene of peple" because her acts of "bisynesse" aided others to understand the faith. "Bisynesse" is presented in all three cases as having a twofold purpose: to keep the individual Christian free from the taints of idleness and to benefit other Christians.[16]

Many of the features of the marriage in the *Second Nun's Tale* are positive ones, and all of them center on the use of the marriage to accomplish good works or "bisynesse." Although Cecilia is not idle at the beginning of the tale, her "bisynesse" is not helping others. She performs what perhaps could be called "bisynesse" by praying to God for the protection of her virginity and by wearing a hair shirt to scourge her flesh when she learns that she must marry Valerian, but these are essentially personal acts. Chaucer shows sensitivity to Cecilia's solitary position at the beginning of the poem by repeating the word "hir" ten times in the first two stanzas to emphasize the "allone"-ness of the maiden, and all her prayers to God at this point in the poem are private ones:

> To God allone in herte thus sang she:
> "O Lord, my soule and eek my body gye
> Unwemmed, lest that it confounded be."
> And, for his love that dyde upon a tree,
> Every seconde and thridde day she faste,
> Ay biddynge in hire orisons ful faste.   (G 135–40)

Chaucer introduces no "frendes" or authoritarian figure to force her into marriage (as do the Middle English analogues) in order to stress her isolated position.[17] Her marriage to Valerian is really her first opportunity to perform acts of "bisynesse" as defined in the prologue.

The marriage dramatically and abruptly changes Cecilia's solitary condition and prods her from her essentially contemplative state into a life of active "bisynesse." The marriage provides a situation in which her good works or "bisynesse" can touch, teach, and benefit others in addition to herself. The wedding night is Cecilia's first act of communion with another person in the poem, and her actions emphasize the solitary state from which she is emerging. She is eager to reveal her "conseil," that an angel protects her, but is hesitant to do so for fear of being "biwreyed" by Valerian. The way Cecilia blends the offer to tell with a fear of telling underscores her own uncertainty or inexperience in reaching out to others, and Valerian's confused and very human reactions to her "conseil" help Cecilia through this first encounter with another human being. Valerian responds to her by demanding to see the angel; otherwise, "And if thou love another man, for sothe/ Right with this swerd thanne wol I sle yow bothe" (G 167–68). But Cecilia persuades him to be baptized by Urban, assuring him that after he is purged from sin, "Thanne shul ye se that angel, er ye twynne." Valerian is baptized and returns to his house, where the spouses are crowned by the angel. Thus, the wedding night is Cecilia's first opportunity to perform "leveful bisynesse," to touch another human being with "clene love." The marriage serves as her introduction to "bisynesse" among humanity, and it initiates a series of acts of "bisynesse" by her and others whom she touches which bring more and more souls into the "cleernesse hool of sapience."

The conversions to a great extent define the value of the marriage of Cecilia and Valerian. Valerian's brother Tiburce is the next to be enlisted in the Christian faith, and his conversion is a direct result of the marriage. The two brothers, in the first fresh exultation of their new-found faith, immediately assume the roles of proselytizers. They are trapped by Almachius' persecution and condemned to be executed. Cecilia visits them in prison and urges them to accept bravely the crown of martyrdom. The bravery they display does in fact result in another conversion, that of Maximus, Almachius' officer; Maximus is also martyred, and his courage in meeting death increases the number of Christians. The final section of the poem describes Cecilia's encounter with Almachius (who is the only character in the poem she cannot convert) and her own horrible death. But throughout her grisly martyrdom she continues her acts of "bisynesse" by preaching the faith to those who are with her and by commending their souls to Pope Urban. Her final prayers, so different from her earliest ones, are general pleas not for an individual human being but for all human beings who will accept the faith. Indeed, her final action is a successful effort to have her earthly "bisynesse" continue after her death: she asks that her house be made a church by Urban to ensure her perpetual "bisynesse" on earth.

Chaucer has chosen to tell the legend in three main sections: the events of the wedding night, the martyrdom of Valerian and Tiburce with Cecilia's parting speech to them, and the martyrdom of Cecilia. The larger progression linking the three sections is the growth of Cecilia as a saint from her first private acts of "bisynesse" in praying for her virginity and wearing the hair shirt to the public "bisynesse" of her final acts. The movement is from Cecilia's thoughts of her own per-fection and salvation to thoughts of the perfection and salvation of others. Her marriage is a liberating and energizing experience for her; it propels her into her career of conversions and martyrdom by giving her a first opportunity to perform "leveful bisynesse."

Donald Howard is correct in drawing attention to some of the posi-tive features of the Cecilia-Valerian marriage. Howard quotes the Par-son, who makes the point that a chaste marriage, when agreed to by the husband, is a "greet merite" for the wife: "And certes, if that a wyf koude kepen hire al chaast by licence of hir housbonde, so that she yeve nevere noon occasion that he agilte, it were to hire a greet merite" (I 945). And in noticing the correspondences between what the Parson commends in marriage and the marriage which occurs in the *Second Nun's Tale,* Howard describes the admirable qualities of Cecilia's marriage: "The marriage here is the vehicle for Christian works and Christian perfection. It is the reverse of the Wife of Bath's voluptuous view of marriage, or of the Merchant's cynical one."[18]

However, as Howard notes,[19] the chaste marriage was not one of the "conseils" which the medieval Church often recommended. In fact, the chaste marriage had been a problematic concern for the Church since the third century. The wives in such a relationship were referred to by any one of a number of unflattering terms (e.g., *agapétae* or *vir-gines subintroductae*). H. Achelis, the modern authority on this sub-ject, traces the unusual custom from its beginning in Apostolic times as it arose from "extreme ascetic motives" to its severe condemnation by the Church in the year 600. The tendency in the development of the custom was for the role of the wife in a spiritual marriage to degenerate from that of "the bride of the soul to that of a housekeeper or occa-sionally a mistress." The high aims of the early Christian ascetics who lived in small communities and were rigidly governed apparently dete-riorated in some cases as the communities grew larger. Achelis notes that the custom "becomes questionable, and even pernicious, as soon as it is made a rule to be followed by a large class of men." In fact the *agapétae* or *virgines subintroductae* did "not practice marriage either in reality or in intention, and were blind to its [the custom's] own dangers, because those who adopted it trusted everything, even the quite impossible, to the power of the Spirit animating Christians."[20]

Although Chaucer's Parson does seem to advocate something like this custom in his "Remedium contra peccatum luxurie," his advocacy ought to be placed in its proper context. The Parson is more than a bit squeamish about the role of sex in marriage,[21] and some of his ideas about sex do not appear in the presumed sources of his tale. Nor do they appear in other late medieval theological works. But even the Parson defines the first and most important reason for marriage as the engendering of children: "for thre thynges a man and his wyf flesshly mowen assemble. The firste is in entente of engendrure of children to the service of God; for certes that is the cause final of matrimoyne" (I 938]. His comments on the idea of *virgines subintroductae* occur in his discussion not of the proper role of the married woman, but of the widow, and some stress must be placed on the list of severe restrictions this kind of relationship imposes on the wife: "Thise manere wommen that observen chastitee moste be clene in herte as wel as in body and in thought, and mesurable in clothynge and in contenaunce; and been abstinent in etynge and drynkynge, in spekynge, and in dede" (I 946–47). Clearly the role of the *virgines subintroductae,* if it could be countenanced at all by the Church of the later Middle Ages, was considered a difficult relationship fraught with potential perils even for the most devout wife.

When we turn to the marriage in the *Second Nun's Tale,* we find a relationship very much like the one the Church cautioned against. In the tale the spouses begin their relationship by swearing to a pact of chastity and accepting crowns which commit them to martyrdom. It is difficult to see how the new relationship that Cecilia and Valerian form can be called a marriage. Rather than a "higher form of marriage" —Howard's phrase—it is a fundamentally different kind of union. The magical wedding night transforms Cecilia and Valerian, like Tiburce, "al in another kynde" (G 252). Chaucer retains the reference to the Ambrosian rite, which is present in the *Legenda Aurea* but not in any of the Middle English analogues, in order to emphasize the transformations which take place.[22] Cecilia literally waives or abandons her marriage—Robinson's translation of "eek hire chambre gan she weyve";[23] Valerian and Tiburce miraculously metamorphose from idol worshipers into Christian activitists. The marriage relationship, which lasts only briefly, is quickly converted into an alliance of the elect.

In fact, as Cecilia grows toward sainthood her marriage becomes less and less important to her. Three of her sequences of dialogue illustrate her rapid progression from cautious and hesitant maiden to self-confident and militant saint; but accompanying her movement toward sainthood we can see the diminishing significance marriage has for her. The first sequence occurs on the marriage night; Cecilia's tone of voice at this point is important, for her manner of speaking characterizes her as cautious and timid before she springs her surprise on Valerian:

> "O sweete and wel biloved spouse deere,
> Ther is a conseil, and ye wolde it heere,
> Which that right fayn I wolde unto yow seye,
> So that ye swere ye shul it nat biwreye."   (G 144–47)

Her tone is filled with almost courtly "gentilesse"; she demurely awaits Valerian's promise not to divulge her "conseil" before she will inform him of it. After Valerian elaborately swears he never will betray her secret, she gains enough confidence to reveal the existence of her guardian angel. This revelation closely follows the rhetorical pattern of the lines just quoted. I have a secret (the angel), and if you promise to do what I ask (love me with "clene love"), I will share it with you ("He wol yow loven as me"). The conditional is the dominant verb tense in Cecilia's speeches; she is testing her conversionary abilities and, as much as the circumstances will permit, gently whetting Valerian's curiosity. Later on the wedding night after Tiburce professes his lack of belief in the efficacy of idols, Cecilia goes so far as to kiss him—though she never kisses her husband—and draw him into the circle of Christian fellowship. Her dialogue in this first long section of the poem is filled with warmth and pious affection for her new converts.

However, the next time we hear her voice she is a changed woman. After the wedding night her next speech occurs at dawn on the day Valerian and Tiburce will be martyred; this is the only time, other than the wedding night, that she speaks to Valerian. She had come to Maximus' house the previous night in order to baptize the officer and his company, but her words appear to be aimed at Valerian and Tiburce:

> "Now, Cristes owene knyghtes leeve and deere,
> Cast alle awey the werkes of derknesse,
> And armeth yow in armure of brightnesse.
>
> Ye han for sothe ydoon a greet bataille,
> Youre cours is doon, youre feith han ye conserved.
> Gooth to the corone of lif that may nat faille;
> The rightful Juge, which that ye han served,
> Shal yeve it yow, as ye han it deserved."   (G 383–90)

How different her voice is here from her earliest speeches on the wedding night. No longer the cautious maiden, Cecilia in her hortatory address attempts to rally the brothers' spirits with martial metaphors. She casts away the conditional tense employed in her first speeches to Valerian, and here she speaks in the imperative mood. However, along with her new, confident tone of voice the decreasing significance of her marriage also becomes clear. She never refers to Valerian, her husband, or Tiburce by name in this her final address to them. The husband-wife bond has been superseded by the relationship of a commander to her troops, urging her Christian soldiers bravely onward. At this crucial point, the impending loss of her husband, Cecilia fails to express the slightest personal concern for their marriage. No word of comfort or love is directed specifically toward Valerian, because their roles as husband and wife have been transcended by their membership in the circle of the elect.

Cecilia's final sequence of dialogue underscores the swift transformation she has undergone from maiden to martyr and from bride of Valerian to bride of God. Her confrontation with Almachius is the climax of the legend; in it she verbally scorns the prefect in belligerent and contentious tones.[24] No longer the shy maiden of the wedding night, she is enflamed with sufficient righteous indignation and combativeness to split hairs with this "lewed officer" and "veyn justise."[25] Self-confident and steadfast, she leaps on every weakness she can find in his speeches and castigates him for his stupidity:

> "O juge, confus in thy nycetee,
> Woltow that I reneye innocence,
> To make me a wikked wight?" quod shee.
> "Lo, he dissymuleth heere in audience;
> He stareth, and woodeth in his advertence!"   (G 463–67)

Never once, however, throughout her confrontation with Almachius does she refer to either Valerian or Tiburce who have only recently been executed by this "Ministre of deeth." By this point in the poem Cecilia has transcended all personal relationships and become an impersonal vehicle for the revelation of divine truth. Indeed, her martyrdom is her institutionalization; her house in which she dies teaching the faith becomes an eternal monument not to her glory but to the glory of the faith. By the end of the *Second Nun's Tale,* Cecilia the woman is lost to Cecilia the saint, and any sense of value in the marriage of human beings has been overwhelmed by the higher goals of martyrdom and conversions.

The marriage in the life of Saint Cecilia probably originally attracted Chaucer to her legend, and at whatever point he thought to incorporate the legend into the *Canterbury Tales,* the decision reflects his usual genius. What other virgin-martyr legend could he have chosen that echoes the ideas of marriage contained in so many other tales and at the same time explores the motivation of a martyr? Too much emphasis in criticism of the *Canterbury Tales* has been placed on determining which tale concludes the marriage discussion or solves the marriage debate. In his Cecilia legend Chaucer approaches marriage from a perspective that is very different from the one he uses in the tales of Kittredge's Marriage Group. The conjugal relationships in the Marriage Group are quite varied, but the spouses are impelled predominantly by Saint Venus; Cecilia is moved by Saint Thomas, to use Arthur W. Hoffman's helpful categorization of motives.[26] The knight and his shape-shifter wallow in their "bath of blisse" at the end of the *Wife of Bath's Tale;* Griselda's crown is made "of many a riche stoon" at the end of the *Clerk's Tale;* January and Arveragus have wives to stroke at the end of the *Merchant's Tale* and *Franklin's Tale* respectively. Cecilia's bath is of divine bliss, and her crown is more precious without rich stones than Griselda's, but Cecilia no longer has a husband. The *Second Nun's Tale* is neither a version of the ideal marriage as espoused by the medieval Church nor a version of the ideal marriage as espoused by Chaucer. Chaucer uses the marriage in the *Second Nun's Tale* to clarify the peculiar rewards and costs of saintliness. He juxtaposes the aim of marriage (the formation of a unique human relationship) against a code of ethics (the extreme Christian faith of the saint) which inevitably denies the basis of marriage by demanding totally selfless dedication to spiritual "bisynesse." What emerges in the tale is neither a denigration of marriage nor a description of the ideal conjugal relationship, but a balancing of the purpose of an earthly calling, marriage, against the goals of a higher calling, martyrdom, which looks beyond all temporal bonds. In the *Second Nun's Tale* the value of human marriage is asserted yet ultimately displaced and overwhelmed by Cecilia's profound saintliness.

NOTES

[1]See Gordon Hall Gerould, "Chaucer's Calendar of Saints," in *Chaucerian Essays* (Princeton: Princeton Univ. Press, 1952), pp. 1–32, for a discussion of Chaucer's references to saints.

[2]All citations of Chaucer's works are from F.N. Robinson, ed., *The Works of Geoffrey Chaucer,* 2nd ed. (Boston: Houghton Mifflin, 1957).

[3]Paul Strohm has described medieval writers' awareness of saints' lives as a literary genre. See *"Passioun, Lyf, Miracle, Legende*: Some Generic Terms in Middle English Hagiographical Narrative: Part I," *ChauR*, 10 (1975), 62–75, and "Part II," *ChauR*, 10 (1975), 154–71.

[4]The following articles demonstrate Chaucer's knowledge of legends associated with saints: John R. Byers, Jr., "Harry Bailey's St. Madrian,"

ELN, 4 (1966), 6–9; Ann S. Haskell, "The St. Joce Oath in the Wife of Bath's Prologue," *ChauR*, 1 (1966), 85–87; Haskell, "St. Simon in the *Summoner's Tale*," *ChauR*, 5 (1971), 218–24; Haskell, "The St. Giles Oath in the *Canon's Yeoman's Tale*," *ChauR*, 7 (1973), 221–26; Daniel Knapp, "The Relyk of a Seint: A Gloss on Chaucer's Pilgrimage," *ELH*, 39 (1972), 1–26. For an interesting discussion of the changing audience for saints' lives (from a primarily monastic audience to a secular one), see Baudouin de Gaiffier d'Hestroy, "L'hagiographie et son public au XIᵉ siècle," in *Miscellanea Historica in honorem Leonis van der Essen* (Brussels and Paris: Éditions Universitaires, 1947), pp. 135–66.

⁵I am indebted to Bertha Ellen Lovewell's *The Life of St. Cecilia*, Yale Studies in English, 3 (Boston: Lamson, Wolffe and Company, 1898) for the information contained in this paragraph.

⁶Lives of these saints are contained in *Jacobi a Voragine Legenda Aurea*, ed. Th. Graesse (Breslau: G. Koebner, 1890). See Margaret, pp. 400–403; Katherine, pp. 789–97; Agatha, pp. 170–74; Lucy, pp. 29–32; and Agnes, pp. 113–17. Ruth Ellis Messenger discusses this group of women saints in *Ethical Teaching in the Latin Hymns of Medieval England: With Special Reference to the Seven Deadly Sins and the Seven Principal Virtues*, Columbia Univ. Studies in History, Economics, and Public Law, No. 321 (New York: Columbia Univ. Press, 1930), pp. 123–25.

⁷Gordon Hall Gerould points out the correspondences between the *Legenda Aurea* version and Chaucer's *Second Nun's Tale* through line 357. See "The Second Nun's Prologue and Tale," in *Sources and Analogues of Chaucer's Canterbury Tales*, ed. W.F. Bryan and Germaine Dempster (Chicago: Univ. of Chicago Press, 1941), pp. 664–84. Gerould believes that Chaucer used a source similar to Mombritius' *Sanctuarium seu vitae sanctorum* after line 357. For a discussion of Chaucer's changes in his sources see F. Holthausen, "Zu Chaucers Cecilien-Legende," *Archiv*, 87 (1891), 265–73; Eugen Kölbing, "Zu Chaucers Caecilien Legende," *Englische Studien*, 1 (1877), 215–48; and Paul E. Beichner, "Confrontation, Contempt of Court, and Chaucer's Cecilia," *ChauR*, 8 (1974), 198–204.

⁸The Middle English analogues are printed in Lovewell (note 5 above), pp. 72–102. For an excellent study of the various versions of Middle English lives of the virgin martyrs see Theodor Wolpers, *Die englischen Heiligenlegende des Mittelalters: Eine Formgeschichte des Legendenerzählens von der spätantiken lateinischen Tradition bis zur Mitte des 16. Jahrhunderts*, Bucht ihe der Anglia. Zeitschrift für eng. Philologie, 10 (Tübingen: Max Niemeyer, 1964), and for comparisons of the Middle English versions contained in *The South-English Legendary* with the *Legenda Aurea* see Manfred Görlach, *The South English Legendary, Gilte Legende and Golden Legend* (Braunschweig: Technische Universität Carlo-Wilhelmina zu Braunschweig Institut für Anglistik und Amerikanistik, 1972).

⁹For additional legends in the *Legenda Aurea* in which the saints refuse marriage offers see Barbara, pp. 898–902; Bridget of Ireland, pp. 902–903; Ursula, pp. 701–705; Petronella, p. 343; and Christina, pp. 419–21.

¹⁰There are no published studies of the refusal-to-marry theme in hagiography; however, a close approximation to this idea can be found in Baudouin de Gaiffier's "Intactam sponsam relinquens. A propos de la Vie de S. Alexis," *Analecta Bollandiana*, 65 (1947), 157–95, which recounts the legends of some 22 saints who renounce their marriages to lead chaste lives.

¹¹The *Second Nun's Tale* contains a dramatic situation which Chaucer will

rework again and again in later tales. The nuptial night is one of his favorite fictional situations. And what we see in this early work is an embryonic suggestion of the later fully developed conjugal-night scenes of the *Merchant's Tale* and the *Wife of Bath's Tale.* Cf. Sheila Delaney's comments on the wedding-night scenes in the *Canterbury Tales* in "Womanliness in the *Man of Law's Tale,*" *ChauR,* 9 (1974), 65–66.

[12]"Chaucer's Discussion of Marriage," *MP,* 9 (1912), 435–67.

[13]On the inclusion of other tales see, e.g., Marie Neville, "The Function of the *Squire's Tale* in the Canterbury Scheme," *JEGP,* 50 (1951), 167–79; and Germaine Dempster, "A Period in the Development of the *Canterbury Tales* Marriage Group and of Blocks B² and C," *PMLA,* 68 (1953), 1142–59. For a rebuttal to Kittredge's argument see Henry B. Hinckley, "The Debate on Marriage in the *Canterbury Tales,*" *PMLA,* 32 (1917), 292–305; for support of the Marriage Group hypothesis see R.E. Kaske, "Chaucer's Marriage Group," in *Chaucer the Love Poet,* ed. Jerome Mitchell and William Provost (Athens: Univ. of Georgia Press, 1973), pp. 45–65.

[14]*MP,* 57 (1960), 223–32.

[15]Joseph E. Grennen, "Saint Cecilia's 'chemical wedding': The Unity of the Canterbury Tales, Fragment VIII," *JEGP,* 65 (1966), 466–81; Paul M. Clogan, "The Figural Style and Meaning of *The Second Nun's Prologue and Tale,*" *M&H,* N.S. 3 (1972), 213–40. See also Edmund Reiss, "Chaucer's Parodies of Love," in *Chaucer the Love Poet,* pp. 27–44. Reiss says, "The *Melibee* is important as a definitive statement of the working of Christian charity, and the Second Nun's Tale is fundamental as a dramatic statement of the ideal marriage," p. 44.

[16]For additional comments on "bisynesse" in the *Second Nun's Prologue* see Mary Giffin, " 'Hir Hous the Chirche of Seinte Cecilie Highte,' " in *Studies on Chaucer and His Audience* (Quebec: For private distribution, 1956), pp. 29–48.

[17]MS. Ashmole 43 has: "þoru hire frendes strengþe; ispoused heo was to a man" (Lovewell, p. 72). MS. Cotton Tib. E. VII (Lovewell, p. 92) has:

> Hir frendes maried hir till a man
> þat named was Valirian;
> Long he was and faire of skin
> And komen of ful nobill kyn,
> Bot hathin he was & unbaptist
> And knew no-thing þe law of Crist.
> Cisill durst none oþer do
> Bot als hir frendes tald hir to.

[18]Howard, p. 229.

[19]Howard, pp. 225–26.

[20]H. Achelis, "Agapétae," *Encyclopaedia of Religion and Ethics* (New York: Scribner's, 1951), I, 177–80. For additional references see Giles Constable, ed., *Medieval Monasticism: A Select Bibliography,* Toronto Medieval Bibliographies 6 (Toronto and Buffalo: Published in Association with the Centre for Medieval Studies, Univ. of Toronto, by Univ. of Toronto Press, 1976), pp. 56–57.

[21]See E. Talbot Donaldson's remarks on the dangers of reading the *Parson's Tale* as a gloss on Chaucer's other tales, "Medieval Poetry and Medieval Sin," in *Speaking of Chaucer* (New York: Norton, 1970), p. 173.

[22]See *Sources and Analogues,* p. 673.

[23]*The Works of Geoffrey Chaucer,* p. 759.

[24]Paul E. Beichner discusses Chaucer's revisions of his source which "intensify the clash between Almachius and Cecilia"; see "Confrontation, Contempt of Court, and Chaucer's Cecilia," pp. 198–204 (note 7 above).

[25]I would like to thank Professor John H. Fisher, who has noticed that Cecilia's character development is comparable to the Canon's Yeoman's character, which progresses from pride in his master's accomplishments to chagrin and eventual anger for what he presents as his almost diabolical mistreatment by the Canon. The Canon's Yeoman joins the Canterbury pilgrimage almost immediately after the conclusion of the *Second Nun's Tale.* For other parallels between the *Second Nun's Tale* and the *Canon's Yeoman's Tale* see Bruce L. Grenberg, "The *Canon's Yeoman's Tale:* Boethian Wisdom and the Alchemists," *ChauR,* 1 (1966), 37–54; Russell A. Peck, "The Idea of 'Entente' and Translation in Chaucer's *Second Nun's Tale,*" *AnM,* 8 (1967), 17–37; Bruce A. Rosenberg, "The Contrary Tales of the Second Nun and the Canon's Yeoman," *ChauR,* 2 (1968), 278–91; and Joseph E. Grennen (note 15 above).

[26]"Chaucer's Prologue to Pilgrimage: The Two Voices," *ELH,* 21 (1954), 1–16.

Morehead State University

JERALD D. JAHN

CHAPMAN'S *ENARGIA* AND THE POPULAR PERSPECTIVE ON *OVIDS BANQUET OF SENCE*

In his recent explanation of the "unnatural perspective" in *Ovids Banquet of Sence,* Raymond Waddington has inadvertently fallen back on an earlier misconstruction of Chapman's artistry. By speaking of the *Banquet* as an exercise in perspectivist illusion, he limits its intended audience to a circle of cognoscenti who understand the poem's esoteric doctrines. In its implications for Chapman's narrative design, such a hermeneutic reading is not far different from that of earlier critics who read the *Banquet* simply as a manifesto "trying to prove that contemplation produced all the delights of the senses," a poem more like a "treatise than a debauch."[1] For them, *Ovids Banquet of Sence* lacked the pleasing *enargia,* or entertaining surface, which should augment the *energia,* or compelling idea, of Sidney's "right" poem and could be read solely for its Neoplatonic theory. Yet, as George Puttenham reminds us, the best poet seeks both to please "by goodly outward shew" and to animate the mind. "That first qualitie the Greeks called *Enargia,* of this word *argos,* because it geueth a glorious lustre and light. This latter they called *Energia,* of *ergon,* because it wrought with a strong and vertuous operation."[2] In his *Banquet,* Chapman clothes the rigorous principles of his philosophy in the luster of a popular and pleasing *enargia* to produce what he calls an "absolute Poem."

There is no reason to question Chapman's philosophical intentions. Neoplatonic ideas obtrude at every joint and motive of the narrative.[3] Rather, the *Banquet* confuses attempts to square its overt philosophizing with its erotically superheated plot. Millar MacLure and J.F. Kermode first noticed that in spite of Chapman's Neoplatonic enthusiasm, neither lover attains an intellectual rapture. James P. Myers,

15

Jr., has seconded Kermode's views, arguing that the poem portrays "Ovid's sensual descent into the lower orders of bestial existence." For Kermode and Myers, Ovid is a "counter-Plato" and Corynna a wanton woman. The natural feasting of their senses leads to a tragic bestiality.[4]

While that view correctly restores the *Banquet*'s narrative quality, questions of Chapman's public intentions remain. For if, as Waddington suggests, Chapman wrote only for an esoteric audience, he must then chastise ordinary readers by offering them a graphic account of Ovid's sexual failure while concealing from them his tragic rationale. That plan seems unnecessarily convoluted—even for George Chapman. MacLure thinks that Chapman may have failed to resolve a personal uncertainty over the paradox of spiritual carnality inherent in Florentine doctrines of love.[5] I think that paradox, whatever its relationship to Chapman's personal reservations, is purposeful in the *Banquet*. From Ficino, Chapman understands that sensual paths to knowledge are problematical at best. The ambiguity inherent in his story of a disrupted sensory feast is intended for readers who have not mastered that paradox through philosophical order.

To clarify Chapman's accommodation of philosophy to a popular perspective, I will offer three propositions concerning his narrative method and its aesthetic intention. First, the *Banquet of Sence* is a vivid, largely sympathetic portrait of a Neoplatonic lover who discovers the limitation of natural reason through erotic experience. Ovid's story is a tragedy of human aspiration which demonstrates Neoplatonic ideas. Second, Chapman models his action principally on short epic techniques and narrative patterns, translating their sensual into his intellectual experience, so as to attract a larger audience through mimicry of a popular form. Third, Chapman's prefatory comments on *enargia* confirm that he wrote for two audiences, one consisting of those who understand Neoplatonic epistemology, the other a "prophane" audience capable of being led to instruction.

Because of its narrative structure, *Ovids Banquet of Sence* is something more than an "oblique attack on the erotic-Ovidian fashion."[6] In effect, Chapman's portrayal of his hero's psychology generates a treatise for learned appetites. Counterbalancing this treatise, however, is a persuasive fiction designed to correct the "muses that sing loues sensuall Emperie." For that purpose, Chapman begins with erotic conventions of the English epyllion. He demonstrates how *enargia,* or "cleerenes of representation," can serve a Neoplatonic "inuention" by encasing Florentine epistemology in minor epic form. Through the persuasive power of a pleasing fiction, Chapman hoped to convince a popular audience that contemporary Ovidian narratives deserved their contempt.

I

Ovids Banquet of Sence embodies philosophy in a dramatic "speaking picture." Chapman conceives his story on three structural levels. Behind discourses on each of the five senses, a linear action follows the legend of how Ovid, "yong in loue," stumbles upon Augustus' daughter in her bath. This history of seduction climaxes when the two lovers touch (st. 110) and are interrupted. Throughout this story, however, Ovid and the narrator provide a second level of commentary on the hero's psyche. Here Chapman takes advantage of a privileged, interior view to enrich events with analysis of their Neoplatonic effects. A third, philosophical and ethical, level of structure governs the sequential ordering of sensual experience. All three "plots" interpenetrate. They overlap in that area of psychological action which correlates Ovid's sensual experience to Neoplatonic epistemology.

Chapman's thematic purpose is usually read in terms of his philosophical structure—the most artificial of his plots. Here, Ovid's movement from hearing, smell, and sight to taste and touch indicates a descending pattern. Sight, although traditionally the purest sense, becomes pivotal, for it supposedly marks Ovid's lapse from contemplative ascent.[7] While Chapman's poem is clearly not a comedy, its narrative action actually involves a double movement. In Ficino, the five senses fall into two groups: those that apprehend beauty without direct physical contact (sight, hearing, and smell) and those which rely on the tangible quality of substance (taste and touch). The latter senses are inferior because they tend to stimulate a desire limited to the material realm; they lead to lust rather than to inspiration.[8] Chapman's arrangement of Ovid's feasting, then, presupposes a theoretical pattern of ascent (to sight) and descent. It comprises a two-part action, a tragedy of aspiration.

Symbolic detail reinforces the *Banquet's* ascending, descending structure. There are, for instance, mythological allusions to human aspirations which end badly; Phaeton, Acteon, Niobe, and Prometheus weave a tapestry of those who attempted too much.[9] In addition, Chapman associates each sense with its operative element: sight works by fire (e.g., st. 66), hearing and smell by air (st. 37 & 39); taste and touch pertain to the earth (cf. *Commentary*, IV, ii; p. 165). Chapman's hero ascends through this hierarchy to fire before plummeting to earth (touch) and, in the emblem of Niobe's fountain which opens the poem, to water. Ovid passes the apex of his ascent through the elements when he discovers that Corynna's kiss effects but a faint echo "of that high joy it worketh in [his] hart." For an echo is nothing but a compression and a thickening of air (st. 100). Chapman's auditory physics signals the turning point in Ovid's amatory ascent.

While such schemes support a tragic view of the legend, Chapman's artistic methods flesh out his purpose. Chapman's central concern is a portrait of Ovid's psychic excitation and disappointment as that action demonstrates Neoplatonic epistemology. To facilitate his interior analysis, Chapman makes both lover and narrator astute, philosophically minded commentators. Chapman's Ovid, though a novice in love, proves a ready student of Florentine doctrine. He learns by experience.

> Neuer was any sence so sette on fire
> With an immortall ardor, as myne eares;
> Her fingers to the strings doth speeche inspire
> And numbered laughter; that the descant beares
>   To hir sweete voice; whose species through my sence
> My spirits to theyr highest function reares.   (st. 17)

Ovid feels the sensuous effects of Corynna's music, her scent, her beauty; from each he intuits the spiritual direction in which his sensual feasting impels him.

> And now my soule in *Cupids* Furnace blazeth,
>   Wrought into furie with theyr daliance:
> And as the fire the parched stuble burns,
> So fades my flesh, and into spyrit turns.   (st. 22)

Throughout the ascending phase of Ovid's courtship, the Roman poet is a high-minded lover. In each rapture he relates sensual gratification to spiritual rarefaction.

Corynna, in turn, embodies a divine effluence of heavenly light. She makes manifest the transporting fire that rarefies a lover in Cupid's alchemical furnace.

> In a loose robe of Tynsell foorth she came,
> Nothing but it betwixt her nakedness
> And enuious light. The downward-burning flame,
> Of her rich hayre did threaten new accesse,
>   Of ventrous *Phaeton* to scorch the fields.
> . . . Then cast she off her robe, and stood vpright,
> As lightening breaks out of a laboring cloude,
> Or as the Morning heauen casts off the Night,
> Or as that heauen cast off it selfe, and showde
>   Heauens vpper light . . . .   (sts. 7, 8)[10]

Initially at least, it is difficult to regard either Ovid or Corynna as simple types of human licentiousness.

Ironic distance between narrator and hero develops relatively late in the action. The narrator maintains one advantage over Ovid, of course —he is at an emotional remove from sensual experiences and can exercise caution in evaluating them. Yet, for much of the poem, it is difficult to detect any difference in philosophical stance between them. The narrator is essentially in sympathy with Ovid's discoveries:

> The sence is giuen vs to excite the minde,
> And that can neuer be by sence excited
> But first the sence must her contentment finde,
> We therefore must procure the sence delighted
> That so the soule may vse her facultie.   (st. 63)

Chapman's Ovid paraphrases Ficino here:

But since the cognition of our minds has its origin in the senses, we should never know the goodness hidden away in the inner nature of things, nor desire it, unless we were led to it by its manifestations in exterior appearance. In this fact is apparent the wonderful usefulness of this beauty and of [love, which is] its associate. (*Commentary,* V, i; pp. 164–65)

Ovid's attempts to satisfy his sensual curiosity are in keeping with Neoplatonic epistemology—to a point. In Corynna's body he glimpses Elysium (see st. 57). With that sight, Ovid ascends as high as untutored experience can carry him; he learns that female beauty is an emanation of heavenly Beauty. Chapman's popular audience has shared vicariously in Ovid's feasting and, through it, in his enlightenment.

Not having read his Ficino, however, Ovid does not know that contemplation alone can carry him beyond this height. Ficino's restrictions on sensual feasting supply a moral comment on Ovid's subsequent attempts to enter paradise.

We are born or reared with an inclination to the contemplative, the practical, or the voluptuous life. If to the contemplative, we are lifted immediately from the sight of bodily form to the contemplation of the spiritual and divine. If to the voluptuous, we descend immediately from the sight to the desire to touch. If to the practical and moral, we remain in the pleasures only of seeing and the social relations. . . . And so all love begins in sight. But the love of the contemplative man ascends from sight into the mind, that of the voluptuous man descends from sight to touch, and that of the practical man remains in the form of sight. (*Commentary,* VI, viii; p. 193)

The senses exercised by Ovid indicate his fall from contemplative aspiration into a voluptuous life. However, his mistake comes less from corrupt desires than from ignorance of Neoplatonic order. From sight, Ovid should have turned to intellectual contemplation.

Disappointed by the temporary rapture of their kiss (st. 100), both lovers push toward a culmination in touch, expecting that last sense to complete their education: "For if wee bee allowd to serue the Eare . . . and to delight the Eye . . . ist immodestie / To serue the sences Emperor, sweet Feeling" (st. 103). Without philosophical study, Ovid and Corynna must reason by analogy. Divine Beauty still infuses Corynna's flesh ("Showing *Latonas* Twinns, her plenteous brests / The Sunne and Cynthia in theyr tryumph-robes / Of Lady-skin" [st. 105]) and retains its power to transport ("And through his Feelings organ to disperse / Worth to his spirits, amply to supply / The porenes of his fleshes facultie" [st. 106]). Like taste, touch is an inferior sense. When the lovers begin to praise it as "King of the King of Sences" (st. 107), the *Banquet* enters an ironic phase. In spite of their high expectations, touch fails to elevate their experience above the merely sensuous or to provide lasting spiritualization.

> But with the tender temper shee was blest,
> Prouing her sharpe, vnduld with handling yet,
> Which keener edge on *Ouids* longings set.   (st. 110)

Chapman's Ovid does not err in his pursuit of knowledge through his senses, but in his ignorance of philosophical order. His concluding lament displays the paradox Ovid has discovered by natural reason, that "a fleshlie engine must vnfold / A spirituall notion" (st. 111). For George Chapman, as for Ficino, only philosophical study can transcend that dilemma.[11] Ovid's keen disappointment gives Chapman's popular reader pause. With Ovid, he must feel the paradox of spiritual longings inherent in the flesh.

While Ovid lacks the knowledge essential to contemplative revelation, Chapman does not blame his hero for attempting to transcend fleshly limitations through natural means. In Ficino, beauty is a sensual bait which attracts all men, and love is the motive by which men are irrepressibly drawn to spiritual discovery (see esp. *Commentary,* VI, ii; pp. 183ff.). When Chapman describes Ovid's aroused emotions,

> So vulture loue on his encreasing liuer
> . . . Wounds him with longings, that like Torrents bleeds,
>   To see the Myne of knowledge that enricht
> His minde with pouertie, and desperate neede:
>   A sight that with the thought of sight bewitcht,
> A sight taught Magick his deepe misterie,
> Quicker in danger then *Dianas* eye.   (st. 41)

he echoes Ficino's description of beauty's enticing effect on the human mind: "By the flames of this beam that natural instinct is kindled; this fire, this ardor rising from its former darkness, from this spark rising to flame is Love born of Poverty and Plenty." He refers to "plenty" because the natural senses feast on physical beauty, and "poverty" because the mind intuits, at each stage of its ascent, the distance between a particular instance of beauty and purer manifestations of Divine Beauty (see *Commentary*, VI, vii; pp. 190ff.). This simultaneous satiety and hunger motivates all men who are attracted to beauty.

The anxiety produced by a Neoplatonic seeker's sense of imperfection is a kind of witchcraft, an enchantment working perpetually in nature through love (*Commentary*, VI, x; p. 199). Chapman's Ovid is motivated by precisely this Neoplatonic psychology. In Corynna's beauty, he desires the image of his own soul as it was, whole and beautiful, in the Angelic Mind (*Commentary*, VI, vi; p. 188).

> This beauties fayre is an enchantment made
> By natures witchcraft, tempting men to buy
> With endles showes, what endlessly will fade,
> Yet promise chapmen all eternitie:
> > But like to goods ill got a fame it hath,
> Brings men enricht therewith to beggerie
> > Vnlesse th'enricher be as rich in fayth,
> Enamourd (like good selfe-loue) with her owne,
> Seene in another, then tis heauen alone.   (st. 51)

When Ovid sells his "freedome for a looke" (st. 50), he obeys the impulse in all men to desire beauty. The simultaneous wealth and poverty of that impulse draws men toward contemplation. Chapman's hero, amid "his fancies storme" (st. 56), is driven by Ficino's psychology of love. He can do little else than follow the allure of sensual beauty. Ovid lacks only the knowledge with which to moderate his ascent at its natural zenith.

Ovids Banquet of Sence, then, is a tragedy of natural aspiration. Chapman no doubt chose Ovid as his hero because of that poet's reputation for licentiousness. But the Neoplatonic psychology which governs dramatic action narrows the ironic distance between hero and narrator; it makes of Ovid an incipient Prometheus, a hero who aspires to great things but cannot overcome natural limitations.[12] Chapman's ordinary readers, enticed by Ovid's vivid psychosensual experiences, arrive with their hero on a scene of frustrated expectations. Ovid complains of the inescapable dilemma of the spirit imprisoned, like a prince, in the flesh:

> O nature how doost thou defame in this
> Our humane honors? yoking men with beasts
> And noblest mindes with slaues?

> . . . and thou that banquests mindes
> Most bounteous Mistresse, of thy dull-tongu'd guests
>   Reapst not due thanks; thus rude frailetie bindes
> What thou giu'st wings; thus ioyes I feele in thee
> Hang on thy lips and will not vterred be.   (st. 112)

Even in his frustration, Ovid pays homage to Chapman's Mistress, philosophy. He has learned the limits of a purely natural love and recognizes that sensory banquets apprehend only a shadow of spiritual beauty. Therefore Ovid vows to make "all fat and foggy braines confesse, / Riches may from a poore verse be deduced" (st. 115) by writing the *Ars amatoria,* presumably as a Neoplatonic poem veiling the "high conceits" that an unlearned poet cannot adequately express. From its close, Chapman's narrative looks outward, to the world of its readers, and suggests that the historical Ovid has become wiser in Chapman's own philosophy. The popular reader should share in Ovid's discovery and recognize his own need for further study.

II

Even for George Chapman, the implication that Ovid discovered Neoplatonic truth is a curious one. We may well wonder if Chapman believed the fiction that Ovid wrote his *Ars* in the spirit of allegory. Chapman's Ovid, who can rail at "these dog-dayes" in which "contagion smoothers / The purest bloods with vertues diet fined" (st. 114), does sound a bit too much like the author himself: "the prophane multitude I hate, & onelie consecrate my strange Poems to those searching spirits, whom learning hath made noble" ("To . . . Royden," *Poems,* p. 49). Seen, however, against a contemporary backdrop of Ovidian short epics which appear to substitute a polished, erotic style for hermeneutic mythography, Chapman's curious invention makes a certain sense. In the *Banquet,* Chapman offers a correction to Ovidian narratives based on an implicit mimicry of their style and structure while staging, as we have seen, an elaborate fictional biography of Ovid's Neoplatonic instruction.

Modern readers of the *Banquet* have often felt its affinity with Marlowe's *Hero and Leander* and Shakespeare's *Venus and Adonis.* Chapman's poem, I think, approaches a generic parody.[13] In his descriptions of Corynna (sts. 7-8; 58-60), for instance, there is enough sensual detail to rival Marlowe's portrait of Leander (I, 51-90) or Shakespeare's figure on Venus as an erotic deer park (ll. 229-40). Further, *Ovids Banquet of Sence* exploits specific narrative formulas characteristic of the Elizabethan short epic.[14] Marlow opens with formal descriptions of Hero (I, 5–50) and Leander, and with a *topographia* on the Temple of Venus (I, 135–57). Shakespeare uses less formal methods of *prosopeia*; he suggests the respective temperaments of his characters, for instance, in images of red and white scattered throughout his action (see, e.g., ll. 35–36; 345–48; 361–66). For his descriptions, Chapman adopts Marlowe's rhetorical formalism in a pyrotechnic portrait of Corynna and an extended depiction of her emblematic garden with its fountain of Niobe (sts. 7–8; 2–6). The art of all three short epics, however, is characterized by the same attention to physical and symbolic detail.

All three also rely on authorial digression. Again, Shakespeare is the least studied artist; his episode of the jennet and stallion (ll. 259–324) seems a coincidence in his fictional world which happens to parallel human events. Marlowe employs a more self-conscious digression, his story of Mercury and the maid (I, 385–484)—a myth within a myth which explains why Hero's prayer will go unheeded. Neither as fanciful as Marlowe's nor as casual as Shakespeare's. Chapman's digression on "natures witchcraft" and "sacred beauty" (sts. 51–55) explains Ovid's compulsion to look in epistemological and psychological terms before returning to the action ("With this digression, wee will now returne / To *Ouids* prospect"). Chapman's digression is a way of alerting his readers to the finer points of Ovid's amorous motivation.

In addition to authorial techniques such as *descriptio* and *digressio,* Chapman shares broader narrative patterns with *Hero and Leander* and the *Venus.* Both earlier poems are stories of seduction. They focus on the events of a single action, lingering over the interplay between two lovers. No one who has read Marlowe can forget his portrait of Hero's coy evasions—her desire to yield, her fear of being counted light. From Shakespeare we recall a darker, but equally analytic, study of female passions and adolescent reticence. Both narratives center on an extended love debate: Leander's love-inspired rhetoric and Venus' fevered persuasions. While Chapman's interest in Neoplatonic psychology displaces it from the center of his narrative, Ovid and Corynna do discuss the tensions between social decorum and spiritual sensuality (see sts. 75–96). For most of his fiction, however, Chapman transforms Shakespeare's analysis of aberrant passion and Marlowe's gnomic asides on human behavior into an extended demonstration of Ficino's theory of human desire.

Of Chapman's two precursors, Shakespeare provides a complete model of short-epic form. *Venus and Adonis* concludes with two tragic events. Nearly the entire final third of the poem explores Venus' reac-

tions to frustration. It is in this final movement, where the legend of
Ovid and Julia grows obscure, that Chapman leans most heavily on
Shakespeare for structural direction. Venus complains against Death
(see ll. 925–1024) and concludes her lament with a curse on love (ll.
1135–64). Thus Shakespeare broadens the etiological sense of the original myth (see *Metamorphoses,* X, 720ff.). His *Venus* becomes a myth
which explains contemporary discord in love. Chapman could hardly
fail to catch Shakespeare's tack. In his legend, Ovid's lament counters
Shakespeare's amorous etiology with a literary one: from his experience, Ovid learned to write veiled, allegorical poetry.

While all the narrative techniques which comprise an Elizabethan
short epic derive from familiar forms of poetry (complaints, the *ques-
tioni d'amore,* seduction poems, and so on), they form a combination
of motifs which is generic. *Ovids Banquet of Sence* resembles that pattern to a degree which suggests that Chapman fused Neoplatonic
analysis to popular form. In doing so, he rewrote the minor epic, cor-
recting its misplaced emphasis on purely natural sexuality. When
Drayton attempted a similar correction in his *Endymion and Phoebe*
(1595), the tragic conclusion implicit in Marlowe's *Hero and Leander*
and realized in *Venus and Adonis* dissolved before Endymion's
dreamy ecstasy. Chapman, guided by short-epic form, retains a tragic
dimension to show readers of epyllia that a merely natural love cannot
enlighten. Chapman illustrates for them that secular love is blind and
must be aided by philosophical knowledge.

Chapman returned to the short-epic genre, of course, in completing
Marlowe's poem. In Chapman's *Hero and Leander* (1598) we find him
again working to correct vulgar interpretations of amorous myth by
erecting on it a philosophical superstructure. There Ceremonie is the
principle of philosophical order which sanctifies secular love. In the
Banquet, however, Chapman tried to play the epyllionists' game for
the sake of his popular audience. As his "Coronet" imitates Petrarchan
sonnet practice, so does his *Banquet of Sence* mimic and transvalue
short-epic naturalism. His success can perhaps be measured by a fellow critic, Henry Reynolds, who in 1632 still rails against mythogra-
phers who study only style:

What can wee expect then of the Poems they write? Or what can a man mee
thinks liken them more fitly to, than to *Ixion's* issue? for hee that with merely
a naturall veine . . . writes without other grounds of sollid learning, than the
best of these vngrounded rimers vnderstand or aime at, what does he more
than imbrace assembled cloudes with *Ixion,* and beget only Monsters?[15]

Chapman might have been more effective in convincing readers that every poet must also be a philosopher had he written a treatise, like Reynold's, on the allegorical nature of classical literature. His legend of how Ovid was initiated into Neoplatonic secrets appears a futile, if not eccentric, corrective to popular fiction.

Yet whatever Chapman may have hoped to accomplish within "the compasse of this curious frame," he wanted it to be that "absolute Poem" which both exploits and transcends popular taste. His prefatory remarks to Mathew Roydon (*Poems,* pp. 49–50) are frequently read as Chapman's defense of an arcane style.[16] While Chapman believed that some Elizabethan readers were of a "wilfull pouertie of iudgements . . . wandring like pasportles men, in contempt of the diuine discipline of Poesie," he does not claim to write in order to preclude understanding. Rather, the letter to Roydon strikes a balance between learning and style which can bring enlightenment to the willing, as well as to the informed, reader. The obscurity Chapman labors to be shadowed in is that of difficult ideas, not of an impenetrable style.

Chapman believes in two classes of receptive readers. The more compatible bring a *furor* akin to the poet's own inspired madness to their reading.[17] In the *Banquet,* this very select audience already understands the philosophical information Chapman dramatizes. "I know, that empty, and dark spirits, wil complaine of palpable night: but those that before-hand, haue a radiant, and light-bearing intellect, will say they can passe through *Corynnas* Garden without the help of a Lanterne" (*Poems,* p. 50). Because of its Neoplatonic content, "varying in some rare fiction, from popular custome," Chapman felt his *Banquet* would prove obscure to the uninitiated.

For them, the poet must provide a lantern. Although its topic should be difficult, the "absolute Poem" avoids unnecessary "obscuritie in affection of words, & indigested concets," finding instead the clearest "fitnes of figure, and expressiue Epethites" with which to express that hard subject. Chapman's poetics operate within a Renaissance definition of fiction's didactic and social purpose. To teach the unwashed, the absolute poem should be delightfully approachable. "That, *Enargia,* or cleerenes of representation, requird in absolute Poems is not the perspicuous deliuery of a lowe inuention; but high, and harty inuention exprest in most significant and vnaffected phrase" (*Poems,* p. 49). Chapman expected some readers to bring a "iudiciall perspective" to his picture of Ovid's amour, a perspective established by Ficino's discussion of philosophical love. At the same time, the absolute poet seeks a "cleerenes" which strikes a midpoint between the "peruiall plainnes" of oratory (which fails to attract and move men) and the childish pedantry of obscurity. This decorous style makes truth available to readers diligent enough to mine it.

With respect to the *Banquet of Sence,* then, Chapman's poetics imply his desire to instill a studious and inquiring attitude in a class of ordinary readers similar to that paradoxical longing for things not seen which Ovid experiences even as his senses are gratified. Chapman's "high inuention" is to depict Ovid as incipient Neoplatonist. In classical logic and rhetoric, "invention" meant collecting arguments and instances appropriate to the case at hand.[18] While Renaissance rhetoricians tended to assign invention to the art of logic, it nevertheless acquired a sense approaching that of fictive creativity.

Stephen Hawes lists five "inwarde wyttes" pertaining to invention. Three (selection of material, "good estymacyon," and "retentyfe memory") are elements of logic and oratory. The other two are more properly creative: "ymagynacyon" and "fantasy." Gascoigne uses invention to mean an original or fresh idea, "some good and fine deuise" with which to express a lyric sentiment. Even though his *Lawiers Logike* (1588) is a treatise on legal oratory, Abraham Fraunce includes imaginative creativity in his definition of invention ("The doctrine of Inuention or Exposition is generall, and not restrained onely to the finding of a Medium [i.e., one of the logical patterns in argument] . . . but absolutely and vniuersally applicable to the inuenting of any thing, either true or fained whatsoeuer"). And Harington nearly duplicates Chapman's sense of invention when he considers poetry as consisting of two operations, "namely inuention or fiction and verse."[19] Half of Chapman's absolute poem, then, consists of a "high inuention"—his fictionalized legend in which Ovid intuits Neoplatonic truth from an affair with Julia. Since that fiction contradicts a popular belief in Ovid's lasciviousness, Chapman expects immediate understanding only from a few, enlightened readers. They will see how his invention challenges the Ovid read in "meerely a naturall veine."

As natural beauty impels men to contemplation through the witchcraft of desire, so, I suspect, Chapman thought delight in his "rare fiction" would motivate untutored readers to search for its philosophical beauty. Chapman's "*Enargia,* or cleerenes of representation" refers to what Harington calls the "clothing or ornament" of fiction. Coupled with *energia,* a persuasive and convincing energy in the poem itself, *enargia* delights so that the subject of the poem may teach. So Puttenham limits *enargia* to the pleasing effects of rhetorical ornament: "And so long as this qualitie extendeth but to the outward tuning of the speach, reaching no higher than th'eare and forcing the Mynde little or nothing, it is that vertue which the Greeks call *Enargia.*" Sidney, however, grafts the pleasing form of fiction, its *enargia,* more firmly onto the persuasive force of its controlling idea:

But truely many of such writings as come vnder the banner of vnresistable loue, if I were a Mistres, would neuer perswade mee they were in loue; so coldely they apply fiery speeches, as men that had rather red Louers writings . . . then that in truth they feele those passions, which easily (as I think) may be bewrayed by that same forciblenes, or *Energia* . . . of the writer.[20]

Poetry is impassioned discourse; its inner energy arouses the mind while its pleasing form impels the emotions. *Enargia,* which attracts an ordinary reader, augments the persuasive discourse of oratory and of fiction.

At the heart of Chapman's letter to Royden lies concern for the poet's didactic responsibilities. For his enlightened readers, an absolute poet provides "that materiall Oration, which [Roydon] call[s] *Schema,* " trusting to their wisdom and skill in perceiving his whole intent. But the absolute poem has its public side as well. Its "significant and vnaffected phrase" attracts the common reader and leads him, through the rich "luster" of its "motion, spirit, and life," to some new understanding. Only the willfully ignorant will fail to see beyond this delightful surface. These "pasportles men" will remain perplexed by Ovid's unfinished banquet.

In *Ovids Banquet of Sence,* Chapman attempts a multileveled absolute poem. At its core is Neoplatonic doctrine—which a privileged few understand "before-hand." But Chapman expects the *energia* of his high invention, a narrative resembling a short epic in form and erotic detail, to attract readers of more popular taste. The tragedy of Ovid's aspirations and his dark hints that "fat and foggy braines" must realize there is more to his poetry than is commonly seen warns those readers against poets who mine a "meerely naturall veine" of erotic mythology. Chapman's ambiguous conclusion leads a popular audience to questions of philosophical order, questions which only a study of Neoplatonic epistemology can answer. If Chapman's Ovid knows that "much more [is] intended," Chapman's popular reader, confronted with his own ignorance, was apparently expected to want to find it out.

NOTES

[1] "An Unnatural Perspective: *Ovids Banquet of Sence,*" *The Mind's Empire: Myth and Form in George Chapman's Narrative Poems* (Baltimore: Johns Hopkins Univ. Press, 1974), see, e.g., pp. 131–37, 141. Muriel C. Bradbrook, *The School of Night* (London: Cambridge Univ. Press, 1936), p. 167, and her *Shakespeare and Elizabethan Poetry* (London: Chatto and Windus, 1951), p. 66; Douglas Bush, *Mythology and the Renaissance Tradition in English Poetry,* rev. ed. (New York: Norton, 1932/1963), p. 212.

[2] Puttenham, *The Arte of English Poesie,* III, iii; in G. Gregory Smith, *Elizabethan Critical Essays,* II (London: Oxford Univ. Press, 1904/1937), p. 148. While Puttenham speaks of *enargia* largely in terms of rhetorical ornament, later Elizabethans like Sidney and Chapman appear to comprehend in the term a vivid portrait of human actions as well, a "speaking picture" which can please in itself and so aid persuasion. On Sidney's understanding of *energia* see Forrest G. Robinson, *The Shape of Things Known: Sidney's Apology in Its Philosophical Tradition* (Cambridge, Mass.: Harvard Univ. Press, 1972), pp. 128–35.

[3] Chapman's sources are variously regarded as Ficino's *Commentarium* (on Plato's *Symposium),* Aristotle's *De anima,* Jean Lemarie de Belge's *Illustrations de Gaule,* and even Barnabe Barnes's *Parthenophil and Parthenope.*

See Frank Schoell, *Etudes sur l'humanisme continental en Angleterre à la Fin de la Renaissance* (Paris: Librairie Ancienne, 1926), pp. 9–14; Jean Jacquot, *George Chapman (1559-1634): sa vie, sa poésie, son théâtre, sa pensée* (Paris: Société d'Edition les Belles Lettres, 1951), p. 65; Bush, *Mythology,* pp. 211–12; and Phyllis Brooks Bartlett, *The Poems of George Chapman* (New York: MLA, 1941), pp. 430–31. Bartlett's edition of the *Banquet* will be cited in the text as *Poems.*

[4] Millar MacLure, *George Chapman: A Critical Study* (Toronto: Univ. of Toronto Press, 1966), pp. 50–59; J.F. Kermode, "The Banquet of Sense," *Bulletin of the John Rylands Library,* 44 (1961), 68–99; and James Phares Myers, Jr., "'This Curious Frame': Chapman's *Ovid's Banquet of Sense,*" *SP,* 65 (1968), 192–206.

[5] MacLure, p. 53. Elizabeth Story Donno also doubts Kermode's thesis, on the grounds that it is too conventional in its interpretation of Chapman's imagery; see her *Elizabethan Minor Epics* (New York: Columbia Univ. Press, 1963), p. 13n. Also, Rhoda M. Ribner, "The Compasse of This Curious Frame: Chapman's *Ovids Banquet of Sence* and the Emblematic Tradition," *Studies in the Renaissance,* 17 (1970), 242; and A.B. Taylor, "Sir John Davies and George Chapman: A Note on the Current Approach to *Ovids Banquet of Sence,*" *ELN,* 12 (1975), 261–65. With MacLure, Enis Rees sees in the *Banquet* a "painful interdependence of flesh and spirit . . . a dilemma that does as much to increase as it does to impair [Ovid's] philosophical zest"— *The Tragedies of George Chapman: Renaissance Ethics in Action* (Cambridge, Mass.: Harvard Univ. Press, 1954), p. 22.

[6] Waddington's phrase, p. 114. For standard views of the *Banquet's* relationship with the short-epic genre, see Hallett Smith, *Elizabethan Poetry: A Study in Conventions, Meaning, and Expression* (Cambridge, Mass.: Harvard Univ. Press, 1964), pp. 88, 96–99; Louis R. Zocca, *Elizabethan Narrative Poetry* (New Brunswick: Rutgers Univ. Press, 1950), pp. 240–43; Donno, pp. 13–16; Bush, pp. 211–13; and MacLure, p. 50.

[7] See Myers, pp. 200–201. There is another, perhaps extraneous, reason for

Chapman placing sight in a central position. Ovid himself described the reason for his exile as an error connected with something he saw, not something he did. See John C. Thibault, *The Mystery of Ovid's Exile* (Berkeley: Univ. of California Press, 1964), p. 29 and *passim*.

[8]Marsilio Ficino, *Commentary on Plato's Symposium*, trans. Sears Reynolds Jayne (Columbia: Univ. of Missouri Press, 1944), I, iv; p. 130—hereafter cited as *Commentary* in the text. See II, iii on the circles, or levels, of being which form a cosmic backdrop for Ficino's epistemology. On touch as the lowest, and bestial, sense, see II, ix; pp. 146–47.

[9]Phaeton, st. 7; Acteon and Prometheus, st. 41. Myers (p. 204) suggests that each of these myths is "expressive of hubris." For a more favorable opinion of Chapman's lovers, see Rees, pp. 21–22; and Ribner, pp. 246, 252, 256–58, who regards Corynna as a mistress-muse suited to Chapman's theme of poetic inspiration.

[10]Ficino explains how corporeal bodies reflect Divine Beauty, the Image of God, in analogies to radiant light (*Commentary*, II, v–vi; pp. 140–41). Through this divine emanation, in its manifold instances, a lover is drawn to God by ascending stages in desire and contemplation.

[11]In his introduction to *Elizabethan Narrative Verse* (Cambridge: Harvard Univ. Press, 1968), p. 18, Nigel Alexander says that while "the claims of passion are recognized in every line of the poem . . . the claim of Reason must still be regarded as paramount." Rees bases Chapman's tragic rationale on his belief in the power of knowledge and contemplation to transcend and order nature; tragedy is a betrayal of that human potential (*The Tragedies of . . . Chapman*, pp. 19-20, 30-31, 179–80). On the importance and sanctity of philosophical ceremony to human love, see D.J. Gordon, "Chapman's 'Hero and Leander'," *English Miscellany*, 5 (1954), 41–94.

[12]In his "Chapman and the Nature of Man," *ELH*, 12 (1954), 92ff., Roy W. Battenhouse suggests that Chapman thought of human potential under three mythic types: Hercules (a figure raging against limitations), Ganymede (an emblem of man's transcendence), and Prometheus (a glorious hero, bound by earthly limitations). Cf. Eugene M. Waith, *The Herculean Hero in Marlowe, Chapman, Shakespeare, and Dryden* (New York: Columbia Univ. Press, 1962), pp. 38, 42-43, and *passim*.

In his "Hymnus in Noctem," Chapman praises the Promethean poet whose "more-than-humane" soul corrects the faults of mankind (see MacLure, p. 38; Waddington, p. 25). Chapman may have conceived of his Ovid as a Promethean hero who becomes the Promethean satirist of the "Hymn."

[13]See MacLure, p. 50; Bradbrook, *Shakespeare and Elizabethan Poetry*, p. 66; Bartlett, p. 5. Although he stresses the importance of generic form in Chapman's poetics, Waddington decides the *Banquet* is Chapman's only non-generic piece (see pp. 10-13, 92-93; 12).

[14]See Paul W. Miller, "The Elizabethan Minor Epic," *SP*, 55 (1958), 31–38. Miller lists the digression, the long speech, "vivid descriptions and strained figures," and a theme of illicit love as generically typical.

[15]Reynolds, *Mythomystes* (London: Henry Seyle, 1632); rpt., Arthur F. Kinney (Menston, Yorkshire: Scolar Press, 1972), C2 (11). As Kinney points out, Reynolds was a friend of Michael Drayton—who wrote the Neoplatonic *Endimion and Phoebe* (1595)—and praised Chapman for his translations from the Greek. *Mythomystes* concludes with "The Tale of Narcissvs, briefly Mythologised," illustrating Reynolds' allegorical approach to the classics.

[16]See MacLure, pp. 45-48; Waddington, pp. 116ff. Charles Kendrick Can-

non argues that in spite of Chapman's opinion of "childish" obscurity, he felt a complicated style necessary to serious poetry. See Cannon, "Chapman on the Unity of Style and Meaning," *JEGP,* 68 (1969), esp. pp. 246-54.

[17]See MacLure, pp. 34-35, who locates the idea's source in Ficino; Jacquot, pp. 212-13; Schoell, pp. 9ff.; Bartlett, p. 2; and Robert K. Presson, "Wrestling with This World: A View of George Chapman," *PMLA,* 84 (1969), 44-50.

[18]See Cicero, *De inventione,* I, vii; trans. H.M. Hubbell, *The Loeb Classical Library* (Cambridge, Mass.: Harvard Univ. Press, 1949), pp. 19-20; and *Ad . . . Herennium,* I, ii, 3; II, i, 1 (trans. Harry Caplan, *Loeb,* (1954), pp. 7, 59). Also, Aldo Scaglione, *The Classical Theory of Composition . . .* (Chapel Hill: Univ. of North Carolina Press, 1972), e.g., p. 141; Charles S. Baldwin, *Renaissance Literary Theory and Practice . . .* (New York: Columbia Univ. Press, 1939), e.g., pp. 53-54, 176; and Donald Lemen Clark, *Rhetoric and Poetry in the Renaissance . . .* (New York: Columbia Univ. Press, 1922), pp. 56-57, 63.

[19]Stephen Hawes, "The Pastime of Pleasure" (1517), ll. 701-63, rpt., William Edward Meade, *EETS,* no. 173 (London: Oxford Univ. Press, 1928), pp. 33-35; George Gascoigne, "Certayne Notes of Instruction" (1575), in Smith, *Elizabethan Critical Essays,* I, 47; Fraunce, *The Lawiers Loglike* (London: William How, 1588), C2v (6v), rpt., R.C. Alston, *English Linguistics, 1500-1800,* no. 174 (Menston, Yorkshire: Scolar Press, 1969); Sir John Harington, "A Preface, or . . . Briefe Apologie of Poetrie" (1591), in Smith, *Essays,* II, 204.

[20]George Puttenham, "The Arte of English Poesie" (1589), Smith, II, 167; Sidney, "An Apology for Poetry," Smith, I, 201. See also Smith's note, II, 419; and Waddington, p. 6.

Vanderbilt University

A.L. AND M.K. KISTNER

THE THEMES AND STRUCTURES OF *A FAIR QUARREL*

In Thomas Middleton and William Rowley's *A Fair Quarrel,* the conflict between appearance and reality—a motif inherent in nearly all of
Middleton's works—passes from its usually subordinate role to dominate the play, providing theme, structure, and unity between the play's
plot levels. The central conflict pits value systems that only appear to
be valid against the one which, in the playwrights' eyes, is genuinely
so. This conflict provides the given situation of the play, and the plot
is contrived as action resulting from the collision between people and
events as they seem and as they truly are. The ultimate outcome of
these conflicts is Middleton and Rowley's statement that certain widely-
adhered-to values (the male code of honor, which was apparently
esteemed by many; the acquisition of material wealth, perhaps less
freely acclaimed but none the less treasured as a guide to conduct; and
indulgence in illicit sexual pleasure, not openly admitted as a standard
of behavior but covertly followed) are false values, the only true ones
being the Christian virtues of love, peace, chastity, and material abne-
gation. Only the pursuit of these values will bring happiness to men.

The playwrights' stance regarding lust and wealth is easily apparent
and excites no comment, being in accord with conventional beliefs
prevalent in their day and our own. Their attitude toward dueling and
the code of honor, however, has not been as easily understood, and
the confusion has led to misunderstanding about the themes and structures of the play.[1]

Like many of Middleton's plays, *A Fair Quarrel* has two structures.
It is organized, first of all, into plot levels: the main plot involving the
Colonel and Captain Ager, the subplot concerning Jane's dilemma,
and a parodic plot level featuring Chough and the Roaring School. In

31

addition, it is structured on the parallel situations of four men, their adherence to false values and their abuse of the women under their authority. The first of these men to be introduced is Russell, to whom wealth is the highest good and the god he will sacrifice his daughter's happiness to: "All my aim is / To cast her upon riches; that's the thing / We rich men call perfection; for the world / Can perfect nought without it" (I.i.10–13).[2] To Russell, the only honor is the deference paid by others to rank gained through riches, and he insists that Jane seek the same goal: "Think of thy preferment: / Honour and attendance, these will bring thee health; / And the way to 'em is to climb by wealth" (I.i.429–31). His devotion to this false god leads to immoral conduct on his part—the wrongful imprisonment of Fitzallen —and imperils Jane's morality as well. She has secretly married Fitzallen but must hide this fact and her pregnancy since she fears her father's certain disapproval (III.ii.49–56). She recognizes two causes for her predicament, her approaching confinement, which will reveal her no longer a maiden, and Fitzallen's imprisonment, which prevents reconciliation with her father and recognition of their marriage; and she lays responsibility for her situation at the feet of the two men in her life, and especially at her father's:

> O my hard fate, but my more hard father,
> That father of my fate!—a father, said I?
> What a strange paradox I run into!
> I must accuse two fathers of my fate
> And fault, a reciprocal generation:
> The father of my fault would have repair'd
> His faulty issue, but my fate's father hinders it:
> Then fate and fault, wherever I begin,
> I must blame both, and yet 'twas love did sin.   (II.ii.56–64)

Thus Russell, through adherence to false values and abuse of his authority over his daughter, commits unethical acts himself and throws Jane into a compromising situation. The peril which confronts Jane in her predicament is her moral downfall, for the Physician, who delivers the baby, demands that she sleep with him to guarantee his silence, and Jane must choose between her reputation, her honor in the world's eyes (and her father's), which she can maintain by appeasing the Physician, and her virtue, maintained by refusing him and being branded a whore when he reveals her child. The Physician's sister succinctly describes the choice that Jane must make:

> Ay, but, mistress, now I consider it,
> Your reputation lies at his mercy,
> Your fault dwells in his breast; say he throw't out,

> It will be known; how are you then undone!
> Think on't, your good name; and they're not to be sold
> In every market: a good name is dear,
> And indeed more esteemed than our actions,
> By which we should deserve it. . . .
> What? do you shrink at that?
> Would you not wear one spot upon your face,
> To keep your whole body from a leprosy,
> Though it were undiscover'd ever? Hang him!   (III.ii.158–69)

Jane decides to repulse the Physician, and thereby she establishes the moral norm for the play. Her choice of true virtue, fidelity to her betrothed husband, over an appearance of virtue which cloaks a hideous vice sets the standard which the characters of the main plot must live up to. By her actions in repelling on the one hand the Physician and on the other her father's attempts to marry her to Chough, Jane rejects both Russell's material values and the values espoused in the main plot, which place honor before the world above virtue.

Parallel to Russell is the Physician, who also abandons his morality and endangers that of his dependent female relation as well. The good which he pursues, however, is sexual satisfaction rather than wealth. In order to satisfy his lust for Jane, he attempts to blackmail her with his knowledge of her child; failing to convince her to yield, he calls in his sister, whose first introduction has been as the near-servant of her brother:

> He is my brother, forsooth, I his creature;
> He does command me any lawful office,
> Either in act or counsel.   (II.ii.70–72)

Anne perfunctorily states that she must persuade Jane "to this act of woman," for as she explains, "I must do my message; / Who lives commanded must obey his keeper" (III.ii.147–49). In other words, Anne is being forced by her brother to act as his pander and to assist him in corrupting Jane. Like Jane, however, she makes the morally correct choice in her dilemma, and after her momentary pretense to be her brother's bawd, she delivers a rousing exhortation that strengthens Jane in her decision. Anne, too, has nearly been forced into immorality by the person presumably responsible for her well-being; and again, the woman has been misused so that her guardian can pursue his own ill-considered ideal.

The third character who follows false ideals to the detriment of himself and of another is Captain Ager, the chief figure of the main plot, whose golden calf is his honor or reputation. His conception of honor is not based on a code of ethics but on the highly formalized dueling code which dealt with the preservation of one's reputation before his fellows more than with morals. According to the code, the defense of one's name when it had been besmirched could only be accomplished by defeating the traducer in the field, and it is over a matter of reputation that Ager and his close friend and fellow-soldier, the Colonel, begin to quarrel. Actually, their quarrel is not even of their own making but adopted from two of their friends whom they discover fighting over whether or not Ager is the Colonel's equal in worth and "manhood." Ager of course feels that he is, while the Colonel believes that his worth is demeaned by comparison to the younger man's.

This disagreement is temporarily smoothed over but breaks out again when the Colonel, further incensed by the wrong done his kinsman, Fitzallen, by Ager's kinsman, Russell, calls Ager the son of a whore, and Ager is sufficiently insulted to demand that they meet on the so-called field of honor. This duel, according to Professor Bowers, is the logical and expected course of action: "That words alone, even such foul ones, would so furiously provoke mortal combat, is dictated by the code of the time whereby a duel for verbal injuries was regarded as sacred in its mission as the judicial combat."[3] It seems apparent, however, that the playwrights disagree with their contemporaries about this reaction to insults. Throughout Act I, scene i, which culminates in the challenge, they have relied heavily on the word *blood* to describe quarreling in terms of wrath which should be quieted. Russell points out that quarreling, like lust, is due to an excess of blood (I.i.52–53); and he and Jane, and even Ager, use the term in their arguments that the anger between the two soldiers should be calmed (I.i.126, 162, 164, 200, 203). For Middleton, who presumably wrote the main plot, overabundant blood and the choler and lust that it breeds is a condition to be avoided.

His belief is expressed again in *The Peacemaker,* a pamphlet printed the year after *A Fair Quarrel* appeared.[4] In it, Middleton writes that "a wise man is free from passion" and exhorts against dueling, particularly against the foolishness of risking life and soul over a verbal insult. The wise man, he insists, disregards insults:

Now the wise and understanding man is not subject or exposed to any of these injuries whatsoever: neither cares he how many darts of malice or contumely are shot against him, since he knows that he cannot be pierced. . . . whatsoever injuries are attempted against a wise man, return without effect, and are to him but as cold or heat, rain or hail, the weather of the world.

And for words of contumely, it is held so small, and so slight an injury, as no wise man complains, or revengeth himself for it.

Duels are based on the "false and erroneous imagination of honour and credit" and "fix their aim and only end upon reputation, and end most lamentably without it, nay, farthest from it: first to hazard the eternal death of their souls, and the surviving bodies to die the death of a cut-purse."

Furthermore, duels are all the more to be deplored when they spill noble and gentle blood, "which, adventured in honorable service, were able to make the fortune of a day, and to change the fortune of a kingdom." In short, it is even worse when the duel "disfurnishes war," that is, when the participants are soldiers.[5]

Middleton continues with several more arguments against the concept of reputation and a declaration of dueling as cold-blooded murder and a sin against the Holy Ghost. He cautions, "Flatter not thy soul then to her everlasting ruin, in thinking reputation consists in blood shedding."[6] He does not present the risks Ager runs in dueling in such harsh terms in the play as he does in the pamphlet (the serious tone of the pamphlet is more appropriate to tragedy than to tragicomedy), but these possibilities of death and damnation were surely in his mind as the duel itself, its outcome, and the comic subplot parodying the dueling code indicate.

This risk of life and soul for a trifle is not, however, the only pitfall before Ager in his pursuit of reputation. Because a particular nicety of the dueling code specified that it is ill for a man to fight in an unjust cause, Ager deems it necessary to question his mother's chastity to be sure that "son of a whore" is indeed an insult and not a statement of fact. Such a questioning is a blatant defiance of the injunction to honor thy father and mother and therefore not only an insult to Lady Ager worse than the Colonel's, since it comes from one so near and dear to her, but also an immoral act. Middleton's attitude toward Ager's great desire to assure himself of his mother's chastity and thereby have good cause to meet the Colonel is reflected in his choice of Ager's diction in contemplation of the duel. "How I thirst for't!" Ager exclaims, anticipating the equally bloodthirsty De Flores' "I thirst for him" (*The Changeling*).

Moreover, the worst of Ager's sin against his mother is the dilemma into which it casts Lady Ager. To think of Lady Ager as under the protection of her young son requires a reorientation in our modern thought patterns, because we generally regard the parent as the figure of authority regardless of sex. But the Elizabethan woman was usually subject to her men—her father, her husband, and then even her adult

son, in the absence of the first two. In Lady Ager's case, this depen-
dency is not only a social convention, but an emotional reality as well;
she is depicted as a doting mother who has no other children, so that
"it follows all the love must come to him" (I.i.36). Her chief desire is
to extract a promise from Ager that he will never again leave England,
and she is characterized as "affectionate," a term which Middleton
often uses to describe a dangerously unreasonable fondness.[7] When
Lady Ager, then, understands that her profession of chastity will send
her son into a duel, she decides to belie her virtue and tell him that he is,
in fact, the son of a whore, fathered by a man other than her husband.

Her decision is sometimes considered a noble one, but she herself
expresses, at great length, the belated belief that it was a poor, if not
an immoral choice:

> Have I belied my faith, injur'd my goodness,
> Slander'd my honour for his preservation,
> Having but only him, and yet no happier?
> 'Tis then a judgment plain; truth's angry with me,
> In that I would abuse her sacred whiteness
> For any worldly temporal respect:
> Forgive me then, thou glorious woman's virtue,
> Admir'd where'er thy habitation is,
> Especially in us weak ones! O, forgive me,
> For 'tis thy vengeance this! To belie truth,
> Which is so hardly ours, with such pain purchas'd,
> Fastings and prayers, continence and care,
> Misery must needs ensue.   (III.iii.20–32)

In addition, her decision has not been worthwhile from even a prag-
matic viewpoint, for Ager simply finds another "cause" over which to
fight the Colonel.

Believing his mother false, Ager feels he cannot righteously meet the
Colonel in the field. He allows his two friends to lead him to the or-
dained meeting place, the "court of justice . . . where all cases of
manhood are determin'd" (III.i.6–7), but assures them he will not
fight. Just as Anne urges Jane to regard what her loss of reputation
will mean, one of his seconds places before Ager what losses refusal to
fight entails:

> Give up your right and title to desert, sir:
> If you fail virtue here, she needs you not
> All your time after' let her take this wrong,
> And never presume then to serve her more:
> Bid farewell to th' integrity of arms,
> And let that honourable name of soldier
> Fall from you like a shiver'd wreath of laurel
> By thunder struck from a desertless forehead,

> That wears another's right by usurpation.
> Good captain, do not wilfully cast away
> At one hour all the fame your life has won.   (III.i.19–29)

But Ager withstands these arguments and declines to defend his honor on false grounds. His decision parallels Jane's in that he forfeits his reputation before the world in favor of preserving what he feels to be true honor in terms of the dueling code. According to Bowers' reconstruction of the code, Ager is behaving as a true Christian in insisting on a just cause for dueling, for "a man who dared to uphold what he knew to be wrong, would be inevitably damned."[8] Clearly, Ager's ethical stance is shown to be superior to that of the blustering Colonel, who is not concerned with truth in any form, only with his reputation. Yet Middleton writes in *The Peacemaker* that peace and contentment, the results of true honor, never belong to the bloodshedder, *"let his cause be never so glorious"* (emphasis ours).[9] In other words, Ager may be a brave and courageous man, living up to the highest ideals of his chosen code, but the code itself is faulted.

Its defects become apparent when the Colonel, seeing that Ager will not fight, calls him a coward, and Ager leaps at the opportunity to defend his "honor" against this insult. His actions pass even the comprehension of his two friends, who can only exclaim, "Should this be true now!" and "Impossible! coward do more than bastard?" (III.i.119–20). Their amazement is probably due in part to their lack of understanding of Ager's fine distinctions, but it cannot help but meet a response in the reader/viewer, whose common sense is astounded by the illogicality of offering to slay or be slain over the insult "coward," particularly after swallowing "son of a whore."[10]

The duel takes place on stage, and it might have been a dramatic piece of action engaging the interest and empathy of the viewer had not Middleton carefully prevented our mistaking the physical valor displayed as worthy of admiration by his provision of a deflating counterpoint in the conversation of Ager's two friends:

> *First Fr. of Cap.* If he should do't indeed, and deceive's
>   all now!
> Stay, by this hand he offers—fights, i'faith!
>   [Colonel *and* Captain Ager *fight.*]
> Fights, by this light he fights, sir!
> *Sec. Fr. of Cap.* So methinks, sir.
> *First Fr. of Cap.* An absolute punto, hey?
> *Sec. Fr. of Cap.* 'Twas a passado, sir.
> *First Fr. of Cap.* Why, let it pass, and 'twas; I'm sure 'twas
>   somewhat.
> What's that now?

Sec. Fr. of Cap. That's a punto.
First Fr. of Cap. O, go to, then;
I knew 'twas not far off. What a world's this!
Is coward a more stirring meat than bastard, my masters?
Put in more eggs, for shame, when you get children,
And make it true court-custard.—Ho, I honour thee!
'Tis right and fair; and he that breathes against it,
He breathes against the justice of a man,
And man to cut him off 'tis no injustice.
                                        [*The* Colonel *falls.*]
Thanks, thanks for this most unexpected nobleness!   (III.i.153–66)

Before the eyes of the viewer is a mortal combat, but at the same time he perceives the inane discussion of whether these deadly blows are "puntos" or "passados." This preoccupation with precious details while men's lives (and souls) are being hazarded reflects Ager's concentration on the niceties of his code when he should be considering whether any insult warrants loss of life or eternal damnation.

Ager's reaction to his infliction of an apparently mortal wound on the Colonel is the self-righteous pronouncement, "Truth never fails her servant, sir, nor leaves him / With the day's shame upon him," to which pomposity his friend replies, "Thou'st redeem'd / Thy worth to the same height 'twas first esteem'd" (III.i.167–69). This answer is open to an ironic interpretation, since the original quarrel was over the esteeming of Ager's worth to be as great as that of the now dishonored, disgraced, and nearly dead Colonel

The sometimes ridiculous and sometimes deadly extremes to which Ager will be driven by his code are not yet at an end, for Lady Ager has by now repented her lie and quickly sets the record straight with her son. He is thankful beyond measure for this reinstatement of her chastity and kneels before his mother, apparently honoring her virtue, but rises only to exclaim that if the Colonel survives his first wound, he will challenge him to a second duel. Lady Ager is utterly defeated by his reaction (IV.iii.83–89), and it is one of the saddest aspects of the play that while her son wrestles with nits, she is subjected to searchings of her conscience, anxieties over her conduct, fears for her son's safety, and emotional traumas that are never truly redeemed in the play, unless the subsequent reconciliation of the Colonel and Ager and the latter's marriage are construed as an easement of her cares over her son's wayward conduct.

Lady Ager is not alone in her incomprehension of Ager's desire to fight the Colonel again; not even Bowers can find reason in the dueling code for his intent.[11] Ager is prevented from this last insanity by a peace emissary from the Colonel, but Middleton has already made his point about the illogical and immoral lengths to which Ager's false code has driven him. Ager, no less than the Physician, has acted immorally to the point of damnation (in the dishonoring of his mother and in the near premeditated murder of the Colonel) and has occasioned the immoral decision of a woman whom he is bound by his male responsibility to protect.

Turning to the Colonel, we find no such subtle treatment of the moral validity of the dueling code as we found in Ager's case. The Colonel is blatantly immoral in his devotion to reputation. To him honor is merely what others think of him, and he will duel to preserve their opinion whatever the cause may be. It is he who first takes offense because his good friend is compared to him in worth and he who will die to defend his insult, "son of a whore," which he must know to be false. His fault, his choleric readiness to take affront and to attack the offender, is again described as an excess of blood. There is a poetic justice discernible to the Colonel in the wound he receives because it punishes the source of his wrongdoing:

> O, just heaven has found me,
> And turn'd the stings of my too hasty injuries
> Into my own blood!   (III.i.176–78)

And the Surgeon who attends him declares that "his principal dolour lies i' th' region of the liver," the seat of the violent passions (IV.ii.14–15).

His wound has a favorable effect on the Colonel, however; it causes him to see what Ager has yet been unable to comprehend—the error of adherence to the dueling code. He recognizes the wrong he has done Ager and hopes to live long enough to win his forgiveness (III.i.178–85). In the meantime, he feels that his spiritual health has never been better:

> I feel an excellent health there [in his soul], such a stoutness
> My invisible enemies fly me: seeing me arm'd
> With penitence and forgiveness, they fall backward,
> Whether through admiration, not imagining
> There were such armoury in a soldier's soul
> As pardon and repentance, or through power
> Of ghostly valour. But I have been lord
> Of a more happy conquest in nine hours now
> Than in nine years before.—O kind lieutenants,
> This is the only war we should provide for!
> Where he that forgives largest, and sighs strongest,
> Is a tried soldier, a true man indeed,
> And wins the best field, makes his own heart bleed.   (IV.ii.44–56)

The choice of military diction in this passage is not only appropriate to the Colonel's character and calling, but also provides a contrast between the physical combat over reputation which the Colonel has previously lost and his current spiritual victory over the powers of darkness. In the tradition of the *Psychomachia* and the morality plays, it is the victory of the virtues over vice. To complete this reformation and to effect what he believes will be a posthumous reconciliation with Ager, he instructs his sister that she will inherit all of his worldly goods and properties if she agrees to give them and herself to Captain Ager. She is most offended at being required to marry her brother's slayer, "one I hate / Beyond the bounds of malice" (IV.ii.81–82), but the Colonel pleads that his soul will never be at peace unless he is allowed to make restitution for his wrongs to Ager through the best means at his command, his sister and his worldly goods. He preaches Christian charity to her and directs her "to love where I forgive" (IV.ii.85–107). Thus the man who once took umbrage at the mere comparison of equal worth is now ready to forgive his murderer and to teach his sister likewise to forget the wrong done to her and to love her enemy. In the first three situations (Russell-Jane, Physician-Anne, Ager-Lady Ager), the woman has been led to the brink of immoral conduct by her male guardian, but the reformed Colonel leads his sister and then Ager to virtuous action.

The sister goes to tender herself to Ager, but he, still bound by thoughts directed by hatred and revenge, expects to receive vituperation from her. "Speak, lady; I'll stand fair," he directs her, as if he were again manfully meeting the foe in the field. He is of course completely disarmed by her kneeling submissively before him and presenting the Colonel's offer. Her kneeling has a thematic significance in its contrast to Ager's kneeling before his mother, which has immediately preceded it. Ager has knelt, as De Flores did before Beatrice in *The Changeling,* seeking a commission to murder, but the Colonel's sister kneels in love and peace, and the result is to undo Ager's "vow" taken at his mother's side. Her love and her brother's love triumph over Ager's hatred.

In the final scene, the two soldiers' rivalry becomes a contest between generosity and love, and their respective seconds are employed as messengers to carry peace offerings back and forth rather than challenges. This, the playwrights indicate, is the only virtuous sparring, and the Colonel's contempt for worldly pelf, his love and forgiveness, and his relation to his sister are established as the true ideals against which Russell, the Physician, Ager, and the Colonel before his reformation must be measured.

Each of the mistaken values exposed in these four character situations is parodied in the subplot activities of Chough, Captain Albo, and the Roaring School. The Roarers' meaningless insults, which result in drinking rather than dueling, imitate the Colonel's and Ager's false values;[12] and Captain Albo's refusal to defend the two whores whom he is paid to protect repeats the dysfunction of male responsibility evidenced in the serious plots. The true worth of Russell's idol, wealth, is exposed in the person of his chosen son-in-law, the rich but simple-minded clown, Chough; and even the Physician's dark desires are ridiculed in Chough's comically coarse wish to wrestle Jane. "The hug and the lock between man and woman," Chough explains, "with a fair fall, is as sweet an exercise for the body as you'll desire in a summer's evening" (II.ii.170–73).

The scene between Chough, Albo, Meg, and Priss (not in the original printing but added later in the same year) asks in comic guise, "What's in a name?" Meg is offended because the captain calls the two girls bawd and whore:

Bawd and whore? out, you unprofitable rascal! hast not thou been at the new play yet, to teach thee better manners? truly they say they are the finest players, and good speakers of gentlewomen of our quality; bawd and whore is not mentioned amongst 'em, but the handsomest narrow-mouthed names they have for us, that some of them may serve as well for a lady as for one of our occupation. (IV.iv.14–21)

Moreover, Priss upbraids him because he does not fulfill his duty to defend the girls when they are insulted as they pass down the street, but Albo only responds with the philosophical question, "What for interjections, Priss?" (IV.iv.6). When the trio meets Chough out to practice his newly acquired Roaring skills, however, Meg and Priss mistake his scurrilities for compliments and placate Albo: "I pray you, captain, be contented; the gentlemen seem to give us very good words" (IV.iv.84–85). The questions being indirectly asked are: Are Meg and Priss not what they are regardless of nomenclature, and is Lady Ager any less virtuous for the Colonel's insult? Has "whore" any more meaning than "bronstrops," "fucus," or "hippocrene"? Will not a rose smell as sweet and skunk weed as unsavory by any other name? To a wise man, has any name enough meaning to risk life and soul for?

The four central situations, then, pit value systems which only appear to be valid against one which is genuinely so. The conflict between appearance and reality which thus underlies the thematic structure of the play also provides the impetus which moves the plot forward, step by step, on each plot level. The conflict is introduced in the opening speech of the play, in which Russell reveals his desire to marry his daughter to a wealthy suitor and his plan to disgrace her preferred lover (I.i.10–25). He has pretended to accept her Fitzallen as his future son-in-law, but he actually means to replace him with another suitor. Russell then compounds his deception by appearing to disarm all the men at his house in the interests of peace, but in reality he is assuring that there will be no interference with his scheme. He admits two men who appear to be testing saltpeter for the king but in fact are bailiffs, and they arrest Fitzallen on false charges. These circumstances precipitate the central conflict of this plot: Jane, about to bear Fitzallen's child, must rely upon the Physician and Anne for the confidential delivery of her baby. She must maintain an appearance of a virginity which has long since ceased to be a reality. The Physician pretends to sympathize with Jane, delivers the baby in secrecy, and then demands his fee: Jane must become his mistress.[13] Jane must choose between keeping the appearance of virtue by losing the reality and keeping the reality by losing the false appearance. At his command, Anne nominally seconds her brother, but in reality supports Jane in choosing true honor, fidelity to her betrothed husband. In addition, the appearance-reality motif is underscored by Jane's castigations of the Physician: "Are you the man / That in your painted outside seem'd so white? / O you're a foul dissembling hypocrite!" She also calls him "thou cinnamon-tree, / That but thy bark hast nothing good about thee!" and "white devil"—all terms expressing the fact that his reality did not live up to his mien (III.ii.102–104, 119–20, 138).

When Jane refuses the Physician, the plot is resolved as it was developed, by a series of incidents pitting appearance against truth. Jane is to be married to the fool, Chough; and the Physician, pretending a sense of man-to-man honor, attempts revenge by telling the prospective bridegroom that she is unchaste. The engagement broken, Russell fakes a reconciliation with Fitzallen, hoping to palm off his honor-stained daughter quickly and quietly. Chough, from a true feeling of honor, tells Fitzallen of the child, and Fitzallen assumes the appearance of wanting nothing to do with Jane. Russell promises a larger dowry, and Fitzallen presents the reality: Russell has been gulled into paying Fitzallen to accept his own wife and child.

The first false appearance of the main plot is the friendship between the Colonel and Captain Ager. Their relationship quickly breaks down when the Colonel feels his honor blemished, and words pass which end in the agreement to duel. When Ager questions his mother to affirm that he is fighting justly, she casts off the reality of her virtue and adopts an appearance of unchastity in order to protect his safety. Ager is now placed in the dilemma of choosing between the appearance of honor, maintained by defending a false cause, or what he believes to be the reality, maintained by refusing to fight and being branded a coward before the world. He meets the Colonel and, apparently seeking to avoid the fight with some remnants of dignity, lectures the Colonel on peace and Christian fellowship:

> 'Tis otherwise with me; I come with mildness,
> Peace, constant amity, and calm forgiveness,
> The weather of a Christian and a friend.
> Thousands have made a less wrong reach to hell,
> . . . .
> Ay, and rejoic'd in his most endless vengeance,
> A miserable triumph, though a just one!
> But when I call to memory our long friendship,
> Methinks it cannot be too great a wrong
> That then I should not pardon. Why should man,
> For a poor hasty syllable or two,
> And vented only in forgetful fury,
> Chain all the hopes and riches of his soul
> To the revenge of that, die lost for ever?
> For he that makes his last peace with his Maker
> In anger, anger is his peace eternally.[14]   (III.i.70–87)

When, however, the Colonel concludes that he is a coward, Ager immediately drops this pretense and begins the duel which "coward" has made him, in his view, morally free to engage in.[15]

After apparently slaying the Colonel, Ager discovers his mother's true chastity and appears to be overwhelmed with regard for her virtue; but in reality, he is intoxicated by the possibility of a second duel (IV.iii.50–80).[16] His joy at this prospect is interrupted by the visit of the Colonel's sister, who appears to Ager to come in war, but who really comes in peace. The quick recovery of the seemingly dying Colonel and the men's reconciliation round off the main plot.

Finally, the appearance and reality theme is supported through the use of the word *fair*. Introduced in the title and repeated throughout the play, *fair* makes twenty-five appearances, usually meaning free from moral stain, generous, promising, pleasing, or direct; occasionally it is used as legitimate, desirable, beautiful, or just. Of chief importance, however, are the instances in which *fair* is used ironically to underline when appearance is not reality. The first of these usages is Fitzallen's greeting to the Colonel, "I gratulate your fair return to peace!" (I.i.144). The Colonel has just returned from the wars and has temporarily patched up his quarrel with the Captain in order to further Fitzallen's suit. The irony lies in the double meaning of *fair,* the apparent definition of pleasing or desirable and the second meaning of specious (*OED, fair,* I,5), since the Colonel's "fair return to peace" will be short-lived. In the second instance, when the supposed saltpeter men are announced to Russell, he bids his servant show them in "by all fair means, sir" (I.i.255), an ironic contrast to the foul means by which the bailiffs are being given entrance. Third, Lady Ager, speaking to her son, refers to the Colonel's "fair goodness" (II.i.46). She is innocently speaking of the Colonel's freedom from moral stain; the ironic meaning intended is his specious goodness, virtue that is only appearance. Jane similarly employs *fair* in speaking of the Physician's "fair condition" or disposition (III.ii.31). She means unblemished, generous, or kind; specious is again more apt. And the Colonel uses *fair* in an intentional oxymoron when he speaks of "fair cunning" (IV.ii.113). He fears his sister is beguiling him and accuses her of practicing what could be the play's keynote, fair cunning, i.e., mean intentions given the appearance of good.

Finally, the Colonel's closing line, "Fair be that quarrel makes such happy friends!" specifies the contrasting, acceptable meaning of *fair* just as it indicates the only allowable kind of quarrel. It reiterates the playwrights' statement on dueling by its implication that any divisive quarrel is infelicitous, and it anticipates a similar statement near the conclusion of *The Peacemaker*: "Why do we quarrel? What is the end of the fairest war? to enjoy peace."[17]

NOTES

[1]Critics have easily recognized the value systems represented in the subplot by Russell (amassing of wealth) and the Physician (satisfaction of lust) as false; but they have usually accepted the values of the main plot, the code of honor or dueling code followed by the Colonel and Captain Ager, as the writers' true ones. Thus David Holmes writes that Ager is "a virtuous young man whom Middleton uses as a moral spokesman" and that Middleton "clearly approves of Captain Ager's readiness to fight for truth" (*The Art of Thomas Middleton* [Oxford: Clarendon Press, 1970], pp. 113, 117). Richard Levin says that Ager's actions set "him above even the noble code . . . of his associates, as the embodiment of male perfection" (*The Multiple Plot in English Renaissance Drama* [Chicago: Univ. of Chicago Press, 1971], p. 69). And Fredson

Bowers compiles elaborate scholarship showing that the Colonel and Ager's quarrel is a "realistic portrayal of the cross-currents of Jacobean thought on duelling" ("Middleton's *Fair Quarrel* and the Duelling Code," *JEGP,* XXXVI [1973], 40). Middleton may have, by research as copious as Professor Bowers' own, made such a graphic presentation of the dueling code; that possibility alone does not, however, justify Bowers' conclusion that "honor and valor, and the strict upholding of these two treasured possessions in strict accord with the contemporary duelling code, are everywhere applauded by the writers and held up for admiration in the speeches of the hero" (p. 64). This traditional view of *A Fair Quarrel* is contradicted by John McElroy, who sets out to prove that the play "treats the hero Ager, as well as the system of values that supports his posturing—namely, the romantic code of honor, which makes male courage and female chastity the supreme values in life" in a manner that is "intentionally parodic" (*Parody and Burlesque in the Tragicomedies of Thomas Middleton,* Salzburg Studies in English Literature, No. 19 [Salzburg, 1972], pp. 266-67).

²This and all subsequent references to *A Fair Quarrel* are from *The Works of Thomas Middleton,* ed. A.H. Bullen (1885; rpt. New York: AMS Press, 1964), Vol. 4.

³Bowers, p. 48.

⁴The British Museum Catalogue ascribes the work to James I, but in the Calendar of Domestic State Papers is an entry for the licensing for printing of *The Peacemaker, or Great Britain's Blessing* by Thomas Middleton. See Bullen, 1, xliv-xlv.

⁵Bullen, 8, 334-36, 338.

⁶Bullen, 8, 339-42.

⁷Lady Ager later castigates her "wretched affection" for guiding her poorly and asks goodness' forgiveness for acting "for my affection's sake" instead of for the sake of virtue (III.iii.19 and IV.iii.35).

⁸Bowers, pp. 51-53.

⁹Bullen, 8, 341.

¹⁰McElroy, p. 305.

¹¹Bowers, p. 63.

¹²Levin believes that the burlesque of the Roaring School applies only to the Colonel, not to Ager, and that Chough "is never allowed any contact with Ager or the Colonel" because it would be "fatal to their refined heroics." Although Chough appears only once in dialogue with Ager, this contact is made through carryover in the viewer's mind and, we feel, is intended to be fatal to the Colonel's and Ager's pretensions (see Levin, pp. 71-72). McElroy also feels that Chough's antics parody both soldiers (pp. 281-83).

¹³The Physician ironically reveals his intent to blackmail Jane when handing the child over to a nurse: "Sweet fro, to your most indulgent care / Take this my heart's joy; I must not tell you / The value of this jewel in my bosom" (III.ii.1-3). These lines complement the theme, since their good appearance disguises their evil intent.

¹⁴These last lines bear comparison with Middleton's remarks in *The Peacemaker,* ". . . and which is worse than madness in those men [duelers], that adventuring to leave this life in anger, presume to press into the next, to the Supper of the Lamb, which is all peace and love, without peace, love or charity" (Bullen, 8, 338).

¹⁵The Colonel's reaction, "Why, he was bookish, / Made an invective lately

against fighting. / A thing, in troth, that mov'd a little with me," is dramatic preparation for his later conversion (III.i.127–29).

[16]McElroy, pp. 315–17.
[17]Bullen, 8, 344.

University of Colorado

DAVID K. JEFFREY

"DUCTILITY AND DISSIMULATION":
THE UNITY OF *FERDINAND COUNT FATHOM*

Critics generally voice two objections to *Ferdinand Count Fathom.*
The first is that the novel juxtaposes narrative elements which are irreconcilable and that its plot, therefore, lacks unity. Thus, for Ernest
Baker, Smollett "confounds the tale of picaresque adventure with
criminal biography; then he changes over to crude romance and the
trials and betrayals of two fond lovers, on to which, for our edification
he patches the absurd conversion episode."[1] Similarly, if more generally, for Lewis M. Knapp "the complete opus does not create a unified
. . . artistic impression."[2] A second critical view finds some unity in
what one of its proponents, M.A. Goldberg, sees as a thematic movement toward a synthesis of Hobbesian art with Shaftesburian nature.[3]
Another, Ronald Paulson, sees a unifying element in Fathom's "five
seductions (or attempted seductions)."[4] But Goldberg finds two flaws
which offset the thematic unity: first, when Fathom battles other villains the results are comic, because the reader feels no sympathy for
either protagonist; while when Fathom battles innocents, the results
are either sentimental or tragic, because the reader feels sympathy for
Fathom's victims. This mixture results in what Goldberg calls "tonal
bifurcation,"[5] which Paulson also remarks.[6] Second, Goldberg cites
four major parts, two distinct climaxes, and Fathom's double rise and
fall as evidence of the novel's "weakness in architectonics,"[7] and
Paulson finds evidence of the same flaw in the shift of the novel's protagonist from Fathom in the first volume to Renaldo in the second.
Like the others, T.O. Treadwell believes the novel an unsuccessful attempt to unite the "irreconcilable" "ethoi of romance and satire . . .,"[8]
and Paul-Gabriel Boucé has called the novel a "failure" because of

47

"the impossible coexistence of picaresque elements side by side with the avowed didactic aim of a moralizing sentimental romance."[9] Their objection here, of course, overlaps with that of the earlier critics; while they grant *Ferdinand Count Fathom* a certain thematic unity with one hand, they deny it unity of plot and tone with the other.[10]

Although I would not argue that the novel is flawless, the book seems to me more unified than these critics recognize. I believe that it is unified by image clusters which reinforce the thematic and structural movement of the work. The primary thematic movement is from appearance to reality, and this progression is manifest in all of the book's narrative threads. I will briefly compare sections of the opening chapters with the last chapter in order to suggest the thematic movement which has taken place between them. Next, I will examine the two major plots to suggest that their developments not only parallel one another, but entwine at significant places. Finally, I will examine the image clusters which reinforce the thematic and structural movement.

I

The narrator generalizes about the appearance-reality theme in the opening paragraph of the novel. Paraphrasing Cardinal de Retz, he remarks on the impossibility of writing an honest autobiography; for, given man's self-interest and self-approbation, man may be "sometimes misled by his own phantasy, and represent objects, as they appear . . . to him, through the mists of prejudice and passion."[11] Man may, in short, mistake what he appears to be, either to himself or to the world, for what he really is. And, of course, the world itself may mistake a man's appearance for his reality. In either case, there is an ironic distance between what is and what only seems to be, a distance to which Smollett gives voice in narrative irony.[12] Smollett assumes the ironic voice in the first sentence of the fourth paragraph, when he characterizes Fathom as a "mirror of modern chivalry" (VIII, 6). Now, while Fathom accurately reflects the concern of some members of his society for the single quality he does not possess at birth, a "tolerable appearance," his only "visible patrimony" (VIII, 6), the ironic distance is evident between the value scale Fathom mirrors, the value scale of "modern chivalry," and the values of true chivalry Smollett suggests in the remainder of the paragraph by pointing out the difference between the origins of the heroes of antiquity and the origins of his own hero; for Fathom is the bastard son of a camp-follower and hardly divine. Nevertheless, the narrator states, Fathom might still "have laid claim to divine extraction" had not his birth been overseen by a veritable army of witnesses (VIII, 7). The ironic distance between Fathom's real origins and the origin he would like to have claimed is couched, appropriately, in ironic language. The paragraph introduces an irreligious villain who bases his character entirely on appearance and on the various guises in which the gullibility of other men makes it possible for him to appear. The ironic tone of the narrative, however, ensures the reader's recognition of the distance between the way Fathom appears and what he really is.

More obvious examples of this ironic expression of the theme occur throughout the early chapters. When Fathom is nine years old, for example, he kisses the hand of the old Count Melvil and prays over him, knowing full well his patron is awake and listening. Fathom thus establishes what "seem[s]" to others "in all appearance" his sense of the Count's goodness (VIII, 25); but Smollett's inclusion of the two qualifying phrases makes clear that Fathom has no real sense of goodness. Similarly, caught plagiarizing a chapter of Caesar's *Commentaries,* Fathom gives "such artful and ambiguous answers" that Renaldo, the Count's son, appears the plagiarist (VIII, 32). Given such skill at twelve years old, the narrator asks ironically, "What might not be expected from his finesse in the maturity of his faculties and experience?" (VIII, 34). Smollett stresses that Fathom's skill is with the "mere exteriors and forms of life," a talent which is "inseparably yoked with the most insidious principle of self-love, that grew up with him from the cradle, and left no room in his heart for the least particle of social virtue. This last, however, he knew so well how to counterfeit, by means of a large share of ductility and dissimulation, that, surely, he was calculated by nature to dupe even the most cautious, and gratify his appetites, by levying contributions on all mankind" (VIII, 29–30). Smollett couches even this explicit statement of the thematic role of his protagonist in bantering and somewhat ironic language.

There is, of course, a difference between what Renaldo appears to be and what he really is, and Smollett also sees this difference ironically; but this irony Smollett directs not against Renaldo but against the society in which he moves, a society which values a "tolerable appearance" above all else. Thus, although in his youth Renaldo shows both scholarly and athletic prowess, the narrator writes, he "at the same time, exhibit[s] such a bashful appearance and uncouth address, that his mother despair[s] of ever seeing him improved into any degree of polite behaviour. On the other hand, Fathom, who [is] in point of learning a mere dunce, be[comes], even in childhood, remarkable among the ladies for his genteel deportment and vivacity . . ." (VIII, 28-29). Similarly, after the plagiarism episode, Fathom manages his answers to Renaldo's father so cunningly that the "old gentleman [is] not satisfied of his son's integrity . . . ; being of a generous disposition, highly prepossessed in favour of the poor orphan, and chagrined at the unpromising appearance of his heir, he suspect[s] that Fathom [is] overawed by the fear of giving offence, and that, notwithstanding what he ha[s] said, the case really [stands] as it ha[s] been represented" (VIII, 33). The Count therefore exhorts his son to benevolence, candor, and generosity, qualities which Renaldo, "under the rough husk of his personal exhibition" (VIII, 33), already possesses. And again in Vienna amidst the social "entertainments," Fathom

soon distinguishe[s] himself by his activity and address, in the course of those exercises that [are] taught at the academy of which he was a pupil; his manners [are] so engaging as to attract the acquaintance of his fellow-students, and his conversation being sprightly and inoffensive, [grows] into very great request; in a word, he and the young Count form . . . a remarkable contrast, which, in the eyes of the world redound[s] to his advantage.

They [are] certainly, in all respects, the reverse of each other. Renaldo, under the total defect of exterior cultivation, possesse[s] a most excellent understanding, with every virtue that dignifies the human heart; while the other, beneath a most agreeable outside, with an inaptitude and aversion to letters, conceals an amazing fund of villainy and ingratitude.   (VIII, 66)

All three examples make clear the direction in which Smollett points his irony. In the first the narrator castigates Renaldo's mother, who does not recognize her son's intellectual and physical superiority over Fathom. In the second the narrator aims his irony at Renaldo's father, who does not recognize his son's moral superiority. And in the third the narrator directs his irony at a world which values Renaldo's virtue less than "the other['s] . . . amazing" manners. Furthermore, in the last sentence of the third example the narrator makes his comments about Renaldo's virtue in a straightforward, nonironic statement, but his remarks on Fathom in the latter half of the sentence, remarks which stylistically parallel the preceding comment about Renaldo, are rendered ironic with the word "amazing."[13] Thus, Smollett structures the whole sentence upon an ironic juxtaposition of a good character not valued by society and an evil character which society does prize; but he employs verbal irony only in the latter half of the sentence in his remark on Fathom. The narrator's comment about Renaldo, as opposed to his voicing of the comments of Renaldo's mother, father, or acquaintances, is not ironic. In short, then, Smollett employs two distinct narrative voices—ironic and straightforward—from the beginning of the novel.

By the conclusion, however, the ironic voice has given way to the straightforward narration of events, and, I contend, this displacement occurs for a thematic reason. For, at the end of the book, a society has been established in which mere appearance is not valued for its own sake and in which, therefore, no distance exists between what a man is and what he appears to be. In the last chapter Smollett draws an explicit comparison between this new social group and the society which it replaces. There, Serafina, accompanied by Renaldo, Don Diego, and Madame Clement, makes her "first public appearance" in London society at an opera:

> the entertainment ha[s] already begun, so that her entrance ha[s] the greater effect upon the audience, whose attention [is] soon detached from the performance, and riveted upon this amiable apparition, which seem[s] to be some bright being of another world dropped from the clouds among them. . . . Every male spectator acknowledge[s] Serafina to be the paragon of beauty; and every female confesse[s], that Melvil [is] the model of a fine gentleman. The charms of the young countess [do] not escape the eye and approbation of royalty itself . . . the fame of her beauty [is] immediately extended over this immense metropolis, and different schemes [are] concerted for bringing her into life. These, however, she resist[s] with unwearied obstinacy. Her happiness center[s] in Renaldo, and the cultivation of a few friends within the shade of domestic quiet. She does not even forget the concerns of the wretched Fathom and his faithful Elenor, who daily enjoy . . . fresh instances of her humanity and care. (IX, 818–19)

The rejection of London society, which values Serafina because of her external beauty, is clear enough. She rejects that society in favor of a social microcosm which prizes real values and in which such meaningful values as "humanity and care" can be expressed. In such a society no distinction exists between appearance and reality: Serafina's physical beauty mirrors an inner spiritual beauty, to which Smollett calls attention by characterizing Serafina as "some bright being of another world dropped from the clouds. . . ." Since in this social microcosm there is no gap between external looks and internal reality, Smollett does not employ the ironic voice which he had adopted earlier to reflect that gap. In short, the novel opens in a world which cannot recognize falsity and closes in a society based on truth; so too the narrative voice shifts to mirror both worlds accurately, the ironic voice becoming less and less evident as the establishment of a society rooted in reality becomes more and more a likelihood.

II

If the theme of *Ferdinand Count Fathom* has to do with the dichotomy of appearance and reality, so also does each of its two plots, as the following brief examination of them will show. My examination of these plots will deal with their thematic and structural progression, and I will suggest that there is a great deal of episodic causality in and between both of them.

Ferdinand's story shows him moving from a world characterized by appearance to one based in reality. Significantly, images of clothing and of disguise most clearly evidence this theme. At the outset, for example, Fathom's "deportment" is "counterfeit" (VIII, 29–30), and he employs "insidious cover" (VIII, 38–39) to deceive others. He extorts money from one of his mistresses by appearing before her "with an air of dejection, which he veil[s] with a thin cover of forced pleasantry . . ." (VIII, 97). After losing his fortune at the hands of Sir Stentor Stiles, Fathom "act[s] the part of a one-eyed fiddler," "covering one eye with a large patch of black silk" (VIII, 186–88). Challenged to duel by a Swiss chevalier, Fathom appears "wrapped up in a long Spanish cloak," reveals the "phenomenon" of a blood-soaked sword, and wins a "sham battle" (VIII, 267–70). He "assume[s] the guise of innocence" when found in bed with Mrs. Trapwell, but because Mr. Trapwell brings him to trial, Fathom's character does not remain "unblemished" (VIII, 300–301). Rescued from prison by Renaldo, Fathom meets Serafina, who has fled her home in Spain and is evading her father's pursuit under the name "Monimia." Fathom attempts to seduce her, first "modell[ing] his features into a melancholy cast, pretend[ing] to share her distress . . ." (IX, 54), and then attempting to rape her.

After her apparent death, Fathom's fortunes begin to decline. Although he would like to "resume the character he had formerly borne in the polite world . . . in any shape" (IX, 109), he cannot do so; for society now recognizes Fathom's imposture. Initially he takes "the title of physician" and assumes its "external equipage" (IX, 112–13), but he must function now at a lower level in society. His decline here is mirrored through a succession of women progressively lower in class:[14] first Miss Biddy and her mother; then a clergyman's wife; next a housekeeper; and then the woman of "very homely appearance," the daughter of a soap-boiler (IX, 155). As he finds himself "descending the hill of fortune," his clothes, aptly, become "rusty" (IX, 154). Finally, in an attempt "to reappear in all his former splendour," he marries Sarah Muddy (IX, 164), and this union completes his descent; it leads to his imprisonment for bigamy and debt. But his misfortune also leads to his repentance: "for the first time, his cheeks [are] bedewed with the drops of penitence and sorrow" (IX, 172–73). When the person of Fathom is next introduced, he is near death: "his face [is] overshadowed with hair and filth; . . . his lips covered with a black slough; and his complexion faded into a pale clay-colour, tending to a yellow hue. In a word, the extremity of indigence, squalor, and distress could not be more feelingly represented" (IX, 300). After reading Fathom's deathbed letter, Renaldo recognizes "there could be no dissimulation or sinister design in this profession of penitence" (IX, 300–302). When Fathom recovers, he presents himself to Renaldo "plainly dressed . . . with his head and body bent towards the earth, so that his countenance could not be perceived," and both his attire and his supplicatory demeanor evidence his repentance (IX, 320). "For all his vice and ambition [are] now quite mortified within him, and his whole attention engrossed in atoning for his former crimes, by a sober and penitent life . . ." (IX, 321). The Fathom plot, then, progresses upward to the attempted seduction of "Monimia" and descends from that peak, ending after Fathom turns spiritually upward in the last two chapters in which he appears.

The Renaldo plot, too, is structured upon the dichotomy of appearance and reality. In significant ways, it simply inverts the Fathom plot. At first Renaldo, as has been shown, has "such a bashful appearance and uncouth address" that his parents despair of him (VIII, 29). Yet, "under the total defect of exterior cultivation" (VIII, 66), he is sensible, virtuous, and honorable. His education in Vienna results in the marked improvement of his "exteriors. . . . All that awkwardness and rusticity, which hung upon his deportment, [is], like the rough coat of a diamond, polished away . . ." (VIII, 125). His appearance no longer masks reality but now reflects it, and he distinguishes himself in social and military life. However, before the prison meeting of Renaldo and Fathom, Renaldo has "retired *incognito* from his family, and travelled through sundry states and countries, in a disguise by which he eluded the inquiries of his parents" (IX, 33). As a consequence of this, his own duplicity, he has left himself open to being "invidiously misrepresented" and excluded from an estate which is really his. His fortunes decline even more rapidly after he introduces Fathom into his household, for he has beggared himself bailing Fathom out of jail, an act which demolishes the "last screen betwixt him and the extremity of indigence and woe" (IX, 45). His effort "to conceal his vexation" produces "a manifest distraction in his behaviour and discourse" (IX, 51), and this "alteration in his countenance" (IX, 52) arouses Monimia's concern. She therefore "over her vexation affect[s] only to give an air of disgust to her internal disturbance" (IX, 56). Both lovers having put on similar appearances, Fathom is able to effect a breach between them, and Renaldo returns to Germany without her.

Renaldo's fortunes, like Fathom's, are reversed after the Monimia chapters. His sister "Removes The Film Which Had Long Obstructed His Penetration, With Regard to . . . Fathom" (IX, 145), and a letter from Monimia has similar results (IX, 211–13). Her letter also causes his delirium and near death; after he fully recovers and is on his way back to London, Renaldo saves Monimia's father, Don Diego, from highwaymen, and the two go to England, where in due course Renaldo is reunited with Monimia-Serafina, not her "phantom," not her "shade," but "the life" (IX, 251), and Don Diego recovers not the "lovely phantom" of Serafina but the "living" woman (IX, 265–66). In the reunion scene Serafina is a "mirror of elegance and beauty" (IX, 264) and, near the conclusion, she is a "pattern of human excellence" (IX, 308), as earlier she has been a "pattern of beauty" (VIII, 203), a "pattern of genuine devotion" (IX, 101), the "fairest pattern of human beauty and perfection" (IX, 172), and a "pattern of constancy and love" (IX, 256). (With such a pattern, Fathom—proposed as a "pattern" by Renaldo's family [VIII, 29 and 65] and believed "the pattern of human perfection" by London society [VIII, 258]—obviously contrasts.) For her wedding Serafina "dress[es] in a sack of white satin . . ." (IX, 284). Neither is there anything "remarkable in the habit of Renaldo, who ha[s] copied the plainness and elegance of his mistress . . ." (IX, 284). Their clothing, like that of Fathom, has metaphorical significance, mirroring their movement toward reality. In the Renaldo plot, then, the complication and resolution are both structured on some aspect of appearance versus reality. In it, as in the Fathom plot, the complication results from the practice of deception, and the resolution occurs only after deception is rejected in favor of reality.

Besides these metaphorical likenesses, there are other specific similarities between the two plots. Perhaps most obvious is the occurrence of four recoveries from near-death, two in each plot, and each of these recoveries acts to bind the plots. It is as if, to proceed to the first of the four incidents, the shot Renaldo fires in a duel with his stepfather, Count Trebasi, has been heard by Fathom, for the consequences of that shot, fired when Fathom is a continent away, cause echoes in the Fathom plot. When Trebasi believes his wound mortal, "all the terrors of futurity [take] hold on his imagination" (IX, 193). Thereafter, "his eyes [are] opened by the danger he ha[s] incurred, and his sentiments turn . . . in a new channel" (IX, 206). Trebasi's near-death and spiritual rebirth hasten Renaldo's recovery of his estate, of his mother, and of his sister; the recovery of the latter is particularly important, for only she, among the characters known to be in Germany, can inform him of Fathom's treachery. Learning of it motivates his desire to return to England "in order to investigate that affair of Monimia" (IX, 207). Renaldo's own near-death and rebirth closely follow Trebasi's. After reading a letter from Monimia, he believes he is responsible for her "death" and falls into a coma (IX, 211–12). Five days later, he nearly dies, but, when momentarily conscious, he expresses his desire to convince Monimia's ghost that he has been, "at least intentionally, innocent of that ruthless barbarity" which has killed her (IX, 216). Motivated by this desire, he recovers and sets out for England. Evidence of his rebirth occurs while he is on the road, where he meets one of Fathom's criminal associates, Ratchcali, but is no longer deceived by him (IX, 222). Renaldo can now see behind the mask of appearance to the reality beneath. Once again the near-death and rebirth have narrative echoes in the Fathom plot. Specifically, when Renaldo sees Fathom on *his* deathbed, *his* face, like Ratchcali's, "overshadowed with hair and filth," Renaldo recognizes Fathom's real repentance (IX, 300). More immediately, Renaldo's near-death and rebirth occasion his journey to England, his consequent meeting with Don Diego, and their reunion with Serafina.

I have already examined Fathom's near-death and rebirth, and only a brief summation should thus be necessary here. Encountering the dying Fathom and believing him repentant, Renaldo asks the clergyman and the physician who have earlier ministered to Serafina to aid Fathom; she concurs in this request, wishing Fathom might "if possible, live to enjoy the benefit of mature repentance, and not die in that dreadful despair which he manifest[s] in the letter" (IX, 302). It is, of course, "possible." Fathom recovers and is truly repentant, saved by their charity and perhaps also by their fervent prayers "that their charity might not be disappointed by the death of the object" (IX, 310). The charity and the prayers of Renaldo and his friends rescue Fathom from a literal and spiritual hell, for if he dies despairing, his salvation is, at the least, not likely. It is not really necessary to point out the way Fathom's near-death and rebirth cause echoes in the

Renaldo plot, since the two narrative threads join in this incident. But such echoes do exist: Fathom's repentance so moves Renaldo that he establishes an annuity for the penitent, and Serafina presents Fathom's wife Elenor with both money and, appropriately, clean linen.

There should be no difficulty either in seeing that Monimia's "death" causes echoes in both plots; it partially motivates the repentances and rebirth of both Fathom and Renaldo. There may be, however, some difficulty in recognizing the need for *her* rebirth, because, like all of Smollett's heroines, Monimia is a good deal less flawed than the other characters. But she does have a flaw, one she shares with Renaldo and Fathom. In London, after Renaldo has bailed Fathom out of jail, he begins "to perceive marks of disquiet and displeasure in the countenance and deportment of his adored Monimia. For that young lady, in the midst of her grief, remembered her origin, and over her vexation affected to throw a veil of tranquillity, which served only to give an air of disgust to her internal disturbance" (IX, 56). She "assume[s] an appearance of disesteem" (IX, 56); her "behaviour [does not] appear" to Renaldo to be "excusable" (IX, 57); and she answers his questions, "summoning her whole pride to her assistance . . . with affected tranquillity, or rather with an air of scorn . . ." (IX, 57). Each beholds "the actions of the other through the false medium of prejudice and resentment" (IX, 58). Tainted by Fathom's machinations, both Monimia and Renaldo begin to play his game; both disguise their real emotions behind affected masks. At her reunion with Renaldo in a cemetery, however, Monimia quite literally "lift[s] up her veil" (IX, 250) and reveals her "pure spirit" (IX, 250), "the warm substance of the all-accomplished Monimia" (IX, 251). And her rejection of London society for "domestic quiet," as has been shown, marks her rejection in a world of seeming and her attempt to establish a world which should be. Indeed, each of the four characters who recover from near-death embraces similar Christian values upon his recovery.

III

Smollett uses other metaphorical word groupings and image clusters which reinforce his theme and structure. One of these has to do with sickness and health, another with Satan and angels. As the novel progresses, Smollett uses more and more images from the second of each of these pairs. As the novel moves toward a "real" world, it also moves toward a healthy and a moral world. Smollett also uses a single cluster of dramaturgical metaphors which supports the novel's thematic movement.

Given Smollett's fascination with the stage, his use of dramaturgical metaphors does not surprise. And of course, such metaphors are particularly appropriate here, given the theme of the novel. Fathom, a master of appearances, prepares for "scenes of life," as an actor prepares for an important role (VIII, 27). He is explicitly an "excellent actor" (VIII, 80), an "exquisite actor" (VIII, 126), and an "inimitable actor" (IX, 105). In the army camp, not content with his role there, he hopes "to act a more important part upon the British scene" (VIII, 132). After stealing Renaldo's jewels, he blames the valet, "perform[ing] his cue to a miracle" (VIII, 134). He is among "the best performers of the age" (VIII, 157), seducing Elenor with an elaborate "dumb show" (VIII, 230), an "expressive pantomime" (VIII, 242), and "act[ing] the part of [her] very importunate love" (VIII, 243). His crony, Ratchcali, has also "acted on the English stage" (VIII, 250) and explains to Fathom the "characters" one might play in that "vast masquerade" (VIII, 253). With Monimia, Fathom prefers to "act . . . the part of young Tarquin" (IX, 98), but, driven from that role at swordpoint, he "resume[s] the character" of physician (IX, 109). Even the prison, as an inmate, Captain Minikin (quoting *As You Like It*) tells Fathom, "is quite a *microcosm,* and, as the great world, so is this, *a stage, and all the men and women merely players*" (IX, 4). Fathom, of course, appears at first only in the villainous roles. However, when he believes himself dying and damned, he (echoing *Hamlet*) calls himself "a smiling villain" (IX, 302). When he later appears to Renaldo, he is "plainly dressed" (IX, 320), no longer in one of his costumes, and the change in his garb manifests his rejection of appearances.

The four near-deaths and rebirths, as has been shown, have metaphorical value also. In each of the four incidents a sick man literally and spiritually becomes well. I want to point out here only that the sickness of Fathom, society, and Renaldo is suggested by other metaphors; that all three recover their health has already been shown. Fathom's sickness is suggested by his loss of "the use of all his limbs" during a rigorous army campaign (VIII, 127), by his "affliction" when caught with Mrs. Trapwell (VIII, 127), and by the "infection" he catches in jail (IX, 110). So too, his sexual appetite is "an infirmity of his constitution" (IX, 157). His "first appearance" in the "external equipage" of the "healing art," his assumption of "the title of physician" (IX, 112–13) is thus ironic—the sick administering to the sick. For society, "infected" by "the spirit of play" which, "like a pestilence, rage[s]" over the land, has a "madness" which Fathom does not even wish to cure (IX, 110–11); indeed, recognizing it, he fosters it, just as he sees how his landlady's "infirmity" is a "disease [that] might be converted to his advantage" (IX, 159). The "sick" Fathom infects Renaldo often, a fact Renaldo recognizes only after his rebirth: "what is life," he then asks Don Diego, "when all its enjoyments are so easily poisoned by the machinations of such a worm!" (IX, 230).

Just what kind of "worm" Fathom is will become clear in the following examination of the novel's religious images and metaphors. These metaphors follow the same pattern already discussed in the examination of the near-deaths; that is, as the novel progresses, the forces of Providence triumph over those of Satan. Smollett first characterizes Fathom as diabolical during an episode in his mistress Wilhelmina's bedroom. Hearing her parents, Fathom hides in a closet, and she "extinguish[es] the light" (VIII, 84). Her father begins his search for the intruder, accompanied by the stepmother "with a light" (VIII, 84). When her father throws open the closet door, the "candle [is] extinguished" (VIII, 86), and Fathom creeps up the chimney. The stepmother returns "with another light" (VIII, 86), and they complete their search. Wilhelmina herself "light[s] another lamp, on pretense of being afraid in the dark," and begins her own search, after her parents have gone (VIII, 86). Unsuccessful, she puts the lamp in the fireplace and in the "gloomy glimmering of the light" gives way to her fear that Fathom is "no other than the devil himself," a belief his appearance from the chimney "begrimed with soot" does nothing to dispel (VIII, 87–88). Indeed, she mistakes "this sable apparition" for "Satan *in propria persona*" (VIII, 88). Smollett's repeated references to the family's difficulties with the light have a broadly comic effect, but they also call attention to his final metaphor—Fathom is Satan, Prince of Darkness. This metaphor is stressed by its repetition in the next chapter, when the father commands "Come forth, Satan" to a wardrobe in his own bedroom in which Fathom is hiding. Immediately thereafter, the father having knocked himself out, the stepmother "put[s] out the light, and in the dark" shows Fathom the way to the door (VIII, 94). In other episodes Fathom is the son of the Pretender (VIII, 231 and 235); learns he can assume various snakelike shapes in which he "glide[s]" and "wriggle[s]" (VIII, 253–54); and is called an "*Angel,*" though not explicitly a fallen one (VIII, 260), a "devil incarnate" (VIII, 270), "diabolical" (IX, 61), "infernal" (IX, 148, 204, and 211), a "serpent" (IX, 203), and the "fiend" (IX, 211). Opposed to him is Serafina, the "seraphic" (IX, 50), the "divine" (IX, 206 and

311), the "superior being" (IX, 250), the "heavenly visitant" (IX, 250), the "ethereal spirit" (IX, 251), the "blessed shade" (IX, 251), the "angel from heaven" (IX, 303), and the "bright being of another world dropped from the clouds" (IX, 318). Serafina's mother likewise was "ever godlike . . . a saint in virtue" (IX, 266). Renaldo too is "sublime," "an angel sent from heaven," Don Diego believes (IX, 227). On his wedding night Renaldo "in a dark passage" sees Madame Clement emerge from Serafina's bedroom "with a light, which, at sight of him, she set down" (IX, 296). This light, however, is "the star that point[s] to his paradise" (IX, 296), rather than, as in Fathom's case, something to be shunned or "ashamed" to face (IX, 313). Light is a metaphor of perception, and Fathom, therefore, shuns the light because in its beams he would be unmasked, his disguise stripped off, his villainy revealed. The clusters around light and dark, angels and Satan, then, reinforce the major theme and reflect its movement.[15]

In summary, the dichotomy of appearance and reality exists not only in the theme and structure of *Ferdinand Count Fathom* but also in the interrelationships of its plots, in its metaphors, and in its images. Smollett stresses this dichotomy in two principal plots which are themselves structured around it, and he uses a variety of metaphorical groupings and image clusters to reinforce his theme.

Such a reading of *Ferdinand Count Fathom* controverts the standard view of the novel's "formlessness," "tonal bifurcation," or "weakness in architectonics" by suggesting that the novel's thematic unity informs and organizes its plots. Such a reading controverts at the same time the widely held view that the novel is picaresque. First, this reading stresses the episodic causality in and between the plots, a principle of causation the picaresque notoriously lacks. Second, this reading points out Smollett's use of different narrative voices to mirror the progress of his plots and his use of carefully developing metaphors to reinforce his theme, neither of which is generally found in the picaresque. Such a reading of the novel, then, indicates that its world is much more tightly organized than the chaotic world of the picaresque —and much more unified than many critics of Smollett believe.

NOTES

[1]Ernest A. Baker, *The History of the English Novel,* IV (London: H.F. & G. Witherby Ltd., 1936), p. 217.

[2]Lewis M. Knapp, *Tobias Smollett: Doctor of Men and Manners* (Princeton: Princeton Univ. Press, 1949), p. 320.

[3]M.A. Goldberg, *Smollett and the Scottish School* (Albuquerque: Univ. of New Mexico Press, 1959), p. 93.

[4]Ronald Paulson, *Satire and the Novel in Eighteenth-Century England* (New Haven: Yale Univ. Press, 1967), p. 228.

[5]Goldberg, pp. 96–97.

[6]Paulson, p. 230.

[7]Goldberg, pp. 97, 99–100.

[8]T.O. Treadwell, "The Two Worlds of Ferdinand Count Fathom," *Tobias Smollett: Bicentennial Essays Presented to Lewis M. Knapp,* ed. G.S. Rousseau and P.-G. Boucé (New York: Oxford Univ. Press, 1971), p. 152.

[9]Paul-Gabriel Boucé, "Smollett's Pseudo-picaresque: A Response to Rousseau's 'Smollett and the Picaresque,'" *Studies in Burke and His Time,* XIV (Fall 1972), 76.

[10]Only Thomas R. Preston finds any unity in the novel. In an exceptional recent essay, "Disenchanting the Man of Feeling: Smollett's *Ferdinand Count Fathom,"* in *Quick Springs of Sense,* ed. Larry S. Champion (Athens: Univ. of Georgia Press, 1974), 223–39, Preston links the work to Fielding's *Essay on the Knowledge of the Characters of Men* and to the whole benevolist controversy as a "problem or thesis novel" in which "Smollett is imposing something like a morality play structure on his familiar fictional world." He argues, however, that Smollett's "characters are instantial throughout the novel, but the scenes are not instantiated until roughly the last quarter of the narration . . ." (pp. 232–33). I will be arguing that Smollett organizes the novel around a different, if related, theme and that the novel is consistently unified throughout.

[11]Tobias Smollett, *The Adventures of Ferdinand Count Fathom, The Works of Tobias Smollett,* The Dalquhurn Edition, ed. G.H. Maynadier (New York: George D. Sproul, 1908), VIII, 5. Subsequent references will be to vols. VIII and IX of this edition and will be cited in the text.

[12]Tuvia Bloch, "Smollett's Quest for Form," *MP,* LXV (1967), 103–13. Bloch calls attention to this irony but believes that Smollett does not sustain it throughout the novel because of his "natural tendency" to state the facts as they are (p. 110). I believe there is a thematic reason underlying the fact that Smollett does not use irony in the latter portions of the book. Cf. Treadwell, pp. 148–51.

[13]Dr. Johnson defines the word in his Dictionary as "wonderful" and illustrates with an ironic remark by Addison on Italy.

[14]Cf. Paulson, pp. 228–30.

[15]Cf. Preston, pp. 232–33, 235–37.

Auburn University

KENNETH W. GRAHAM

IMPLICATIONS OF THE GROTESQUE: BECKFORD'S *VATHEK* AND THE BOUNDARIES OF FICTIONAL REALITY

We all know that art is not truth. Art is a lie that makes us realize truth, at least the truth that is given us to understand. The artist must know the manner whereby to convince others of the truthfulness of his lies.

Pablo Picasso[1]

A central concern of modern criticism of *Vathek* is the apparent failure of Beckford to find a suitable style for his theme.[2] Martha Pike Conant, for example, admires the "impressive catastrophe" in the scenes of Vathek's damnation but regrets "the mockery, the coarseness, and the flippancy" in the body of the narrative which seem inappropriate to a Faustlike quest for power and knowledge.[3] James Rieger alleges that Beckford failed to reconcile wit and context in *Vathek*: "But to be really effective [wit] must appear to arise from its own context; what surprises the reader should also generate its own internal logic. Beckford fails entirely to accomplish this."[4] Those critics who postulate an artistic (and moral) disjunction in *Vathek* do not understand that Beckford has established an original aesthetic perspective which, if perceived and understood, reveals not a fissure in *Vathek* but an extraordinarily interesting fusion of contraries. Walter Allen is on the right track when he emphasizes the peculiar nature of the wit in *Vathek*—"a fabulous wit depending on the juxtaposition of the unexpected . . . to produce the bizarre or grotesque image"—and the peculiar content from which that wit arises—"fantasy . . . rooted in the perception of the real."[5] By applying the perspectives of the grotesque to fiction to create a fictional world that blends the fantastic and the real, Beckford extended the boundaries of fictional reality in a

61

way that represents a response to the concerns and an advance on the practice of his contemporaries. The perspectives of the grotesque range (in Ruskin's language) from the "sportive grotesque" to the "terrible grotesque"; it is the range of the grotesque that allows Beckford to create a world of irrationality and amorality and so cast doubt on (in Yeats's language) "this pragmatical, preposterous pig of a world" portrayed in the novel from its beginnings to the present. As Donne was misunderstood and dismissed for so long because the originality of his technique was not properly appreciated, so with Beckford. Beckford's originality lies in his forging a new perspective that can indeed reconcile such disparates as the sublime and the grotesque, the moral and the amoral, the fantastical and the real. *Vathek,* properly understood, employs a vital reconciliation of style and theme to create an impressive expansion of fictional reality and an unusually powerful tale.

In a work published in 1762, Bishop Richard Hurd reflected on a revolution in aesthetics that he thought had taken place about one hundred years earlier. Hurd's revolution saw the birth of a conception of Nature as "the known and experienced course of the affairs in this world" flourishing over the dead ashes of the poetic notion of a "magical and wonder-working" nature.[6] The revolution saw a triumph in literature of empirical conceptions of probability and the defeat of the gothic and faery imagination that Hurd found in the works of Shakespeare and Spenser. Hurd concludes his study, *Letters on Chivalry and Romance,* on a wistful note: "What we have gotten by this revolution, you will say, is a good deal of good sense. What we have lost, is a world of fine fabling. . . ."[7] The wistfulness is itself a symptom of a counterrevolution of which Hurd was perhaps conscious, a counterrevolution dominated by a spirit calling for a return to romance, a spirit demanding an extension of the boundaries of reality, particularly in the realm of prose fiction.

Firmly in the spirit of this Romantic counterrevolution is the gothic novel *The Castle of Otranto* (1764), Horace Walpole's attempt to introduce romance into prose fiction. His preface to the second edition expresses a similar aesthetic regret at the limitation on imaginative resources imposed by an age of reason. Walpole's novel endeavored to redress the balance between reason and imagination; he called his work

an attempt to blend the two kinds of Romance, the ancient and the modern. In the former, all was imagination and improbability: in the latter, nature is always intended to be, and sometimes has been, copied with success. Invention has not been wanting; but the great resources of fancy have been dammed up, by a strict adherence to common life.[8]

Walpole's preface expresses the dichotomy to be reconciled in terms of a number of contraries, among them the following: the supernatural and the natural, the improbable and the real, the sublime and the naïve, imagination and historical accuracy. It is unfortunate that in the case of *The Castle of Otranto* a shadow falls between the conception and the creation. However admirable Walpole's aim to free the imagination through a blending of the modern and the ancient romances, his means are at times ludicrous: the imagination is not appropriately engaged by a statue with a nosebleed or a portrait that sighs. Judging from the results, Walpole's ancient romance embraces ghosts, solemn processions, a villain-hero derived probably from Jacobean melodrama, and a sprinkling of "low" characters; his conception of modern romance adheres strictly to current notions of sensibility. Walpole's gothic vehicle, impelled by self-conscious supernaturalism, steered by uncertain villainy and unevenly laden with moral weeping and virtue rewarded, soon bogs down in bathos. *The Castle of Otranto,* however significant its aims, fails for lack of a technique for fusing the old with the new.

The limitations imposed on imaginative literature that Walpole and Hurd acknowledged presented a serious problem to an age that prided itself on being reasonable. Should the common experience of everyday life be used to judge the validity of imaginative experience? Hurd points out that since 1660 the conventional answer to that question had been "yes," and, as a result, "a world of fine fabling" has been lost. But the age of Hurd and Walpole was not an age reconciled to the answers that satisfied previous generations nor to an acceptance of the losses those answers entailed. Rather, it was an age of experiment, experiment not confined to such as Priestly, Watt, and Wilkinson, but extending to painting with the water-color techniques of Alexander Cozens, to architecture with the gothic adornments of Strawberry Hill, to atmospheric poetry with Macpherson and Chatterton, and to prose fiction with *Tristram Shandy*. That these and many other manifestations of an unwillingness to be limited by past accomplishments in art were accepted by the public demonstrates an ethos current in the mid to late eighteenth century represented by a readiness to accept experiment and novelty.

William Beckford's *Vathek* (1786) is an unusually apt manifestation of the period of aesthetic experiment and uncertainty through which English art and letters were passing during this time. It presents as fine

a fable as any that Hurd was wistfully recalling; it introduces supernatural machinery and a hero-villain just as Walpole did, although
Beckford's supernatural is more faerie than gothic; and it presents the
bizarre tale of the Caliph Vathek with the puckish humor and enlightened good sense associated with an age under the influence of Dryden,
Swift, and Pope. All the characteristics that Walpole ascribed to the
ancient and modern romances are to be found in *Vathek*. The supernatural and the natural are blended in a cast of characters that includes Mahomet and Eblis and their respective servants, the Genius
and the Giaour at the supernatural level, as well as a host of people
who bear an unmistakable humanity, sometimes staggering under its
burden and sometimes delighting in its variability. The episode of
Vathek's thirst blends the improbable and the real: what could be
more extraordinary than Vathek's unquenchable thirst induced by
magic, yet, after he had done nothing for days but drink to excess,
what could be more natural than Vathek's desire after his cure to eat
to excess? The human characters range from low to high, from the
sweating, breathing populace of Samarah to Vathek himself, combin-
ing in his position of caliph the functions of emperor and pope.
Naïveté is found in the behavior of the fifty children, unknowing sac-
rificial victims; sublimity in Vathek's displays of magnificence. Imagination and historical accuracy are blended at the base of the tale, an
entry in D'Herbelot's *Bibliothèque Orientale: Vathek* is an imaginatively embellished biography of an historic personage.

Although the characteristics of *Vathek* just outlined show a consciousness of the problem of aesthetic limitation troubling Walpole and
Hurd, Beckford's solution to the problem represents a considerable
advance over their thinking. What is significant is not the presence of
Walpole's contraries in Beckford's tale but rather his use of appropriate techniques to achieve an aesthetic reconciliation of these disparates
as well as an unusual vision of reality consonant with the techniques.
Broadly speaking, the sublime and the grotesque are the two categories of writing from which to draw techniques appropriate to the
reconciliation of the empirically plausible and the imaginatively improbable. While Beckford makes use of the sublime in *Vathek,* more
frequently he draws upon techniques of the grotesque to reconcile the
disparates of fantasy and reality and answer the problem of aesthetic
limitation.[9]

The nature of the reconciliation of fantasy and reality achieved by
techniques of the grotesque is less a blending than an incongruous and
ironic fusion of these disparates on the fictional spectrum.[10] This

strange fusion of these two qualities in the grotesque is the outcome of a particular vision of the world. The grotesque world is one that disobeys the laws of nature: in visual art it is a world in which animals resemble plants, or men animals, a world that violates the precepts of nature separating mineral, vegetable, and animal. Projections of this world of physical abnormality result in affective characteristics that involve, according to Ruskin, an early theoretician on the subject, a blending of the ludicrous and the fearful.[11] Depending on the element that predominates, the forms of the grotesque can be ranged on a spectrum, the extremes of which are, in Ruskin's terms, the sportive grotesque in which the ludicrous predominates, and the terrible grotesque in which the fearful predominates.

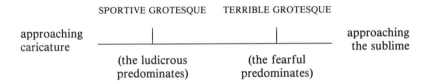

The use of techniques of the grotesque leads to the projection of a vision of reality that is profoundly disturbing. Not only does the employment of grotesque techniques evoke simultaneously a response of amusement and terror, but the world that is projected presents an ominous combination of the familiar and the alien that disorients the observer. To create a grotesque world is to cast doubts upon a rationally conceived, ordered, law-obeying nature.

A number of scenes, characters, and incidents presented in *Vathek* contain elements of the grotesque. Some examples fall clearly into Ruskin's category of the sportive and others into his category of the terrible. The constituents of these examples demonstrate either a fascination with physical abnormality or a particularly creative tension of the ludicrous and the terrifying: in either case the employment of the grotesque leads to a perception of the human condition as diminished. Beckford's use of the grotesque has a number of implications, in particular regarding his solution to the aesthetic problem posed by Hurd and Walpole, but also concerning the tradition of the prose romance and Beckford's part in that tradition. To consider the operation and implications of Beckford's use of elements of the grotesque leads also, almost inevitably, to wider concerns, since to use techniques of the grotesque is to create a strange and sinister form of fictional reality. The recognition of the moral and aesthetic significance of that sinister reality leads to an awareness of the unusual breadth of vision in *Vathek* that establishes for Beckford a special place in the history of prose fiction.

Among the figures populating the pages of *Vathek* are a surprisingly large proportion of the physically grotesque. There are "fifty female negroes mute and blind of the right eye"[12] who are particularly talented in the use of the garrotte. Beckford offers us also this description of another strange assortment of people, the objects of the charity of the Emir Fakreddin:

> Wherever the Caliph directed his course, objects of pity were sure to swarm round him; the blind, the purblind, smarts without noses, damsels without ears, each to extol the munificence of Fakreddin, who, as well as his attendant greybeards, dealt about, gratis, plasters and cataplasms to all that applied. At noon, a superb corps of cripples made its appearance; and soon after advanced, by platoons, on the plain, the completest association of invalids that had ever been embodied till then. The blind went groping with the blind, the lame limped on together, and the maimed made gestures to each other with the only arm that remained. The sides of a considerable water-fall were crowded by the deaf; amongst whom were some from Pegû, with ears uncommonly handsome and large, but who were still less able to hear than the rest. Nor were there wanting other, in abundance with hump-backs; wenny necks; and even horns of an exquisite polish.   (61–62)[13]

What is significant in this passage is not the description of physically abnormal creatures, but the manner in which the description is presented. The particular fascination with the physically abnormal gives rise here to a tension between the comical and something else that jars with merriment. Beckford presents this spectacle in a form of derisive burlesque that assaults our humanity. We are entertained and disturbed: the martial imagery in this context amuses us, but because we are amused we are also repelled by the lack of charity both in the description and in ourselves for being amused. There seems also to be a quantitative dimension to Beckford's employment of the grotesque. To present one or two grotesque personages might be amusing or disturbing enough, but Beckford's canvas teems with grotesques. Not only does he offer platoons of invalids but also a succession of scholars proudly sporting interminable beards, two pious dwarfs who recite the Koran monotonously and endlessly (they are reciting it for the nine hundred and ninety-ninth time in the course of the tale), the abnormally fat and conceited Bababalouk, Vathek's chief eunuch, whose voice resembles "the ringing of a cracked jar" (58), and an unusually large number of silly, decrepit, and pious graybeards. One has a disturbing feeling that the examples of humanity in the tale take pride in the extent of their own deformity and are bent on adding to their own abundant store of natural grotesqueness and absurdity.

A character who assumes special significance in this context is the Giaour (or infidel), who appears as a merchant of magical wares. He is described as "so abominably hideous that the very guards, who arrested him, were forced to shut their eyes, as they led him along" (5). When he laughs, he discovers "his long amber-coloured teeth, bestreaked with green" (6). Later, when Vathek is about to express his displeasure with him in the form of a hearty kick, the Giaour rolls himself into a ball, whereupon Vathek, his court, and the whole populace of his capital are impelled by magic to join in an undignified and one-sided soccer match, following in the wake of the rolling Giaour, all endeavoring to address a few kicks at the ball but for the most part receiving kicks from one another. Here is part of the account:

The shrill screams of the females, who had broken from their apartments, and were unable to extricate themselves from the pressure of the crowd, together with those of the eunuchs jostling after them, and terrified lest their charge escape from their sight; the execrations of husbands, urging forward and menacing each other; kicks given and received; stumblings and overthrows at every step; in a word, the confusion that universally prevailed, rendered Samarah like a city taken by storm, and devoted to absolute plunder.   (19–20)

The influence of the Giaour distorts human behavior and intensifies the natural absurdity of the people. Thus, in presenting the physically grotesque, Beckford emphasizes the element of behavior rather than mere physical characteristics. Grotesque behavior may have an internal cause, such as pride, or an external agent, such as the Giaour, the servant of Eblis, the Satan of Muslim demonology. In both cases, the grotesque is associated with evil and represents disorder at the physical and moral levels of existence.

To employ physical disorder to reflect moral chaos is a traditional technique in literature, and such a conjunction of physical and moral chaos is inherent in techniques of the grotesque. But within the grotesque spectrum are two extremes, the sportive and the terrible: the intensity with which moral disorder is communicated will depend on which extreme of the spectrum is employed. In employing the sportive grotesque, Beckford places emphasis on the physical chaos of his fictional world while suggesting that the chaos extends to the moral levels of existence. To focus his emphasis on moral disorder he turns to the terrible grotesque, employing darker techniques in which the fearful predominates in its tension with the ludicrous. The world reflected by the terrible grotesque is sinister in its lawlessness, since that lawlessness is perceptible at the ethical and moral levels of existence. It is a world apparently bereft of moral significance, a world in which good and evil seem rewarded or punished in accordance with no plan. The portrayal of such a world would approach the sublime in its fearfulness were it not transformed by an element of the ludicrous.

That element of the ludicrous that Beckford employs to hold the portrayal of fearful scenes within the realm of the grotesque is the device of the sardonic narrator, the source of the flippant tone that has so exasperated commentators. The function of the narrator can be demonstrated in a number of scenes. For example, on one occasion, partly from natural inclination and partly to obtain directions, Carathis, Vathek's mother, finding herself near a cemetery, decides to summon the ghouls which inhabit such regions, using the dead bodies of her guides to tempt their appetites. The account continues:

[T]he surface hove up into heaps; and the ghouls, on all sides, protruded their noses to inhale the effluvia, which the carcases of the woodmen began to emit. They assembled before a sarcophagus of white marble, where Carathis was seated between the bodies of her miserable guides. The Princess received her visitants with distinguished politeness; and, supper being ended, they talked of business.   (92)

The tension here is between the terrifying nature of the ghouls and their revolting act of eating corpses on the one hand and, on the other, the ironic reserve of the narrator, demonstrated in his choice of the conventional expression, "supper being ended, they talked of business." Most of the shocking excesses presented in the tale are narrated in a similar tone. Vathek's attempted sacrifice of fifty beautiful children to the appetite of the Giaour, the murder in the tower of one hundred and forty men attempting to rescue Vathek from what they think to be a dangerous fire, Vathek's sacrilege in fouling the sacred broom carried to him by pilgrims from Mecca, all are narrated in a tone of restrained amusement, sympathizing neither with the victims nor with the perpetrators of vicious acts but encompassing all with sardonic observations. The discrepancy between style and content forces an uncomfortable fusion of the ludicrous and terrifying. The assumption of normalcy inherent in the tone creates in the reader an ethical disorientation. The world presented has no apparent moral meaning, yet the ambivalence of the narrator's ironic reserve will not permit that conclusion to be drawn.

By using techniques of the grotesque, Beckford was able to reconcile the attributes of Walpole's ancient and modern romance reflected in Hurd's two realities, "the known and experienced" and the "magical and wonder-working." The leap from the experienced to the magical is accomplished by the tension between the ludicrous and the fearful inherent in the grotesque. In employing the sportive grotesque to present the experienced world, Beckford transforms fictional reality by distorting character and behavior. In *Vathek,* the empirical world is overly real: Vathek, in building five palaces for the titillation of each of the senses, is too sensual, the populace is too gullible, the Emir, the pilgrims, and the dwarfs too pious, and the long-bearded scholars too pretentious. The empirical world has residual characteristics that make the setting recognizable as our conventional world, but added to it is a foreign dimension, a strangeness that carries it into the "magical and wonder-working." The employment of the terrible grotesque casts a sinister gleam on the blend of reality and fantasy in Beckford's fictional world. He presents extremes of vicious behavior but in his narration understates those extremes, or directs the attention of the narrative to aspects of behavior one would not normally emphasize. The result of this sinister juxtaposition of reality and fantasy is a disorientation that forces the reader to question the limits convention imposes on reality.

While Beckford extends the boundaries of reality, he also extends the limits in which moral judgment can operate. Beckford's fictional world functions *apparently* without moral law, yet the commentary on occasion suggests that moral meaning may be found beneath the ostensible chaos. Note the moral comment implied in this description of the fate of the one hundred and forty men seeking to rescue their caliph whom they believe to be threatened by a fire:

In fact, these good people, out of breath from ascending fifteen hundred stairs in such haste; and chagrined, at having spilt by the way, the water they had taken, were no sooner arrived at the top, than the blaze of the flames, and the fumes of the mummies, at once overpowered their senses. It was a pity! for they beheld not the agreeable smile, with which the mutes and negresses adjusted the cord to their necks: these amiable personages rejoiced, however, no less at the scene. . . . They all fell, without the least resistance or struggle: so that Vathek, in the space of a few moments, found himself surrounded by the dead bodies of the most faithful of his subjects. . . .   (34–35)

The folly of the men is demonstrated in the absurd futility of their act. There is no dangerous fire in Vathek's tower, only a pyre to propitiate the powers of evil. Even if there had been a need for rescue, the men would have been useless since in laboring up the stairs of the tower they had lost all the water they carried. To extreme futility is added extreme callousness: the selflessness of the men is repaid by cruelty; their lives are taken from them. This description presents a world of futility, alienation, and meaninglessness. Yet, despite the apparent lack of meaning in the world, it is possible to make a moral judgment. Certainly one is implied in the account just quoted. Present with the sardonic cruelty of the tone, particularly in the ironic "It was a pity!", is a quieter voice heard in the last sentence of the passage: "Vathek, in the space of a few moments, found himself surrounded by the dead bodies of the most faithful of his subjects. . . ." The moral judgment residing in that voice suggests that a meaningful order exists beyond the chaotic patterns of human behavior.

Beckford makes use of the grotesque in *Vathek,* then, to link empirical reality with imaginative reality. The grotesque, characterized by absurdity and ominous distortion, confers a sense of the uncanny on empirical reality; its use suggests the inadequacy of empirical conceptions. The effect of Beckford's employment of the grotesque is to disorient the reader. On the one hand, the lightly ironic tone used to present acts of viciousness perpetrated upon ludicrous creatures suggests to the reader that neither the acts nor the victims are to be taken seriously. On the other hand, the necessity of a moral judgment, suggested in some of the descriptions, is confirmed in the account of the fate of Vathek and his mother. In punishment for their cruelty, they are condemned to eternal torment. Thus, while extending the limits of reality using techniques of the grotesque, Beckford extends also the area in which a moral judgment must operate.

It is interesting to observe that two hundred years after the complaints of Hurd and Walpole on the restrictions of fictional reality, Angus Wilson, surveying the development of the novel since Richardson and Defoe, comes to similar conclusions. In an article published in the *Kenyon Review* in 1967 entitled "Evil in the English Novel," Wilson laments the restrictions that English novelists have traditionally placed on their form. He traces the source of the restriction to the eighteenth century, when evil almost disappears from the novel as a result of the influence of Fielding and Smollett. Transcendent questions of good and evil which he finds in Richardson's *Clarissa* become transformed into questions of propriety, or correct and incorrect behavior. With Jane Austen, Wilson continues, "[a] middle-class view of right and wrong is considered sufficient to explain human conduct."[14]

Certainly one of the weaknesses of Walpole's *The Castle of Otranto* is its lack of a sense of evil. The supernatural in the novel is associated with the rights and wrongs of social stability: specifically, supernatural agents act to effect the return of a piece of property to its rightful proprietor. The god of *The Castle of Otranto* is an upholder of the traditional social order based on land and blood, a god that someone of the social standing of Horace Walpole might find it advantageous to believe in.

The use of the grotesque in *Vathek* calls attention to the presence of evil pervading the natural and supernatural worlds. In the natural world the seeds of disorder are present in each individual, and when nourished with pride or malice they spring forth in grotesque and distorted forms of behavior. In the supernatural world perhaps the most apt image of disorder is the palace of the fallen angel, Eblis, where the architectural harmony of "rows of columns and arcades" (109) is rendered dissonant by the chaotic wanderings of the damned.

> In the midst of this immense hall, a vast multitude was incessantly passing; who severally kept their right hands on their hearts; without once regarding any thing around them. They had all, the livid paleness of death. Their eyes, deep sunk in their sockets, resembled those phosphoric meteors, that glimmer by night, in places of interment. Some stalked slowly on; absorbed in profound reverie: some shrieking with agony, ran furiously about like tigers, wounded with poisoned arrows; whilst others, grinding their teeth in rage, foamed along more frantic than the wildest maniac. They all avoided each other; and, though surrounded by a multitude that no one could number, each wandered at random, unheedful of the rest, as if alone on a desert where no foot had trodden. (109–10)

Eblis himself reflects the disorder of his palace in his tarnished beauty and his blended serenity and despair.

Hurd's two realities are joined inadequately by Walpole because he limits the supernatural by making it uphold a conventionally accepted social order. Beckford uses the grotesque in *Vathek* to demonstrate the limitations of a world in which Christianity has become reasonable and reality empirical, a world in which questions of good and evil have dwindled into questions of right and wrong. *Vathek* affirms the existence of evil not as a negation of good but as a powerful and independent force of disorder.

To extend the spectrum of the grotesque beyond the terrible so that the result contains no element of the ludicrous is to approach the sublime. The sublime and the grotesque have two similar attributes: they employ sensual objects to evoke a reality beyond the sensual, and their projection of that reality is tinged with terror. The two differ in the nature of the reality beyond the sensual that they project. The reality evoked by techniques of the sublime is characterized by a powerful and mysterious unity and order; the reality projected through the grotesque is chaotic and lawless. In *Vathek* the separation of good from evil is enhanced by contrasting the techniques of the sublime and the grotesque. The good, represented by Mahomet and his servant, the shepherd-genius, are presented in terms of the sublime; the evil, Eblis and his servant, the Giaour, are presented in terms of the grotesque. The grotesque is thus seen in contrast with the sublime: seeing and understanding all is Mahomet in his seventh heaven (but all is not right with the world); the shepherd-genius plays a compelling and awesome music and presents Vathek with a dire warning that Vathek courageously but foolishly ignores. The contrast between the sublime and the grotesque is a contrast between order and anarchy, kept separate at the cosmic level but confusingly intermixed at the mundane. The evil of Eblis and his palace is evoked through techniques of the grotesque to demonstrate the confusion within the supernatural world. That confusion is magnified at the mundane level, a *chiaroscuro* world, nocturnal and fantastic, isolated from sublime order and goodness by the existence of the grotesque, which darkens all aspects of behavior and alienates human beings from the ideals their worthiest representatives would be governed by.

That constricted conceptions of reality have imposed limitations on literature is a complaint of a range of thinkers from Hurd in the eighteenth century to Wilson in the twentieth. The development of prose fiction from the romance of the sixteenth and seventeenth centuries to the novel of the eighteenth century records a progressive narrowing of fictional reality that culminates in the novels of Jane Austen. Walpole attempted to check this process of restriction by introducing supernatural agencies into the world of his fiction, but his technique is too mechanical and his conception of fictional reality too narrow for his vision to carry much conviction. Beckford improved upon Walpole by employing the grotesque to accomplish an organic fusion of the natural and supernatural levels of reality. Beckford extends the boundaries of fictional reality much more vitally than Walpole because his conception of this reality is more mysterious and ominous. His experiment with the grotesque led, perhaps inevitably, to the presentation of evil as the mysterious force bridging the supernatural and the natural, for Beckford's reality is not only a reflection of sublime order but also, through his emphasis on physical abnormality and the disturbing fusion of the ludicrous and the terrifying, a reflection of an ominous disorder. Having faced the individual with a reality more chaotic and unpredictable than conventional notions have indicated, he faces man also with the responsibility for moral decision in a world that seems to reward evil.

The significance of Beckford's experiment went unrecognized in the mainstream of prose fiction in the nineteenth century, but the quality of Beckford's accomplishment can be measured with reference to Picasso's statement about art in the epigraph. Beckford had the vision to present a reality not quite recognizable as the reality that common sense has decided is the only practicable one, yet it is a reality that the imagination has already experienced. He has distorted conventional reality in order to present a different reality in which the individual is isolated from order and evil is a real and independent force. In creating an uncommon yet plausible reality, a disturbing yet engaging structure of the imagination, Beckford has used the grotesque "to convince others of the truthfulness of his lies."

NOTES

[1]Pablo Picasso, "Art as Individual Idea," *The Arts,* 3 (May 1923), 315–26. Text here is from Richard Ellmann and Charles Feidelson, Jr., eds., *The Modern Tradition* (New York: Oxford Univ. Press, 1965), p. 25.

[2]A number of critics avoid the problem by focusing merely on style. Edmund Wilson ascribes the irony not at all convincingly to a need on Beckford's part "to satisfy a perverse impulse" (*The Shores of Light,* p. 266), and James Folsom sees in the style of *Vathek* and *The Episodes* "a satire on some of the absurdities of the Oriental tradition" ("Beckford's *Vathek* and the Tradition of Oriental Satire," *Criticism,* 6 [1964], 54).

[3]M.P. Conant, *The Oriental Tale in England in the Eighteenth Century* (1908; rpt. New York: Octagon Books, 1966), p. 62.

[4]J.H. Rieger, "Au Pied de la Lettre: Stylistic Uncertainty in *Vathek,*" *Criticism,* 4 (1962), 306.

[5]Walter Allen, *The English Novel* (New York: Dutton, 1954), p. 91.

[6]Richard Hurd, *Letters on Chivalry and Romance,* ed. Edith J. Morley (London: H. Frowde, 1911), p. 138.

[7]*Ibid.,* p. 154.

[8]Horace Walpole, *The Castle of Otranto,* in Peter Fairclough, ed., *Three Gothic Novels* (Harmondsworth, Middlesex: Penguin, 1968), p. 43.

[9]An interpretation of Beckford's reconciliation of disparates may be found in my paper, "Beckford's *Vathek*: A Study in Ironic Dissonance," *Criticism,* 14 (1972), 243–52. The present paper represents an extension of the earlier interpretation.

[10]A large number of modern studies of the grotesque are available. I found the following works particularly useful in preparing this paper: Wolfgang Kayser, *The Grotesque in Art and Literature,* tr. Ulrich Weisstein (New York: McGraw-Hill, 1966); Philip Thomson, *The Grotesque* (London: Methuen, 1972); and Michael Steig, "Defining the Grotesque: An Attempt at Synthesis," *Journal of Aesthetics and Art Criticism,* 29 (1970), 253–60.

¹¹John Ruskin, *The Stones of Venice,* in E.T. Cook and Alexander Wedderburn (eds.), *The Works of John Ruskin* (London: G. Allen, 1904), XI, 151.

¹²William Beckford, *Vathek,* ed. Roger Lonsdale (London: Oxford Univ. Press, 1970), p. 31. Subsequent page references to this edition will be given in parentheses after the quotation.

¹³Also quoted by Allen in *The English Novel* (pp. 91–92) as an example of Beckford's "fabulous" wit.

¹⁴Angus Wilson, "Evil in the English Novel," *Kenyon Review,* 29 (1967), 171.

University of Guelph

JOHN K. CRABBE

THE HARMONY OF HER MIND: PEACOCK'S EMANCIPATED WOMEN

"To think is one of the most unpardonable errors a woman can commit in the eyes of society," says Anthelia Melincourt, heroine of Thomas Love Peacock's second novel, *Melincourt* (1817). She continues her lament:

In our sex a taste for intellectual pleasures is almost equivalent to taking the veil; and though not absolutely a vow of perpetual celibacy, it has almost always the same practical tendency. In that universal system of superficial education which so studiously depresses the mind of woman, a female who aspires to mental improvement will scarcely find in her own sex a congenial associate; and the other will regard her as an intruder on its prescriptive authority, its legitimate and divine right over the dominion of thought and reason. (188)[1]

Anthelia has only slightly overstated the case. Assertively intellectual herself and well educated in the classics, she finds no companions among women and few men willing to grant the validity of her arguments. Yet in the end, without abandoning either her intellect or her femininity, she garners the reward of Peacockian comedy, marriage with the man of her choice, a husband who will respect her rights and powers.

Anthelia's success marks the emergence in Peacock's work of the type of independent and assertive woman who was to figure frequently in his subsequent fiction. Writing at a time when authorial approval went more frequently to delicacy and submission, Peacock produced a series of learned and sprightly women who provide a delightful counterpoise to his own babbling philosophers and to the faint and fainting heroines of gothic fiction. He is, as Walter Allen has noted, "one of the few men novelists between Fielding and Meredith who can draw a satisfying woman."[2]

75

The satisfaction of Walter Allen and others with Peacock's women deserves closer study, because Peacock is usually read not for his development of character but for his mockery of absurd ideas carried to extremes. His extravagant conversations among riders of assorted hobby-horses result in a fiction which resists classification. For Northrop Frye, Peacock provides a paradigm of the anatomy, that comprehensive species of fiction that deals "less with people as such than with mental attitudes."[3] Frye grants that Peacock is "as exquisite and precise an artist in his medium as Jane Austen is in hers,"[4] but such emphasis obscures the fact that, like Austen's, Peacock's plots always lead to the altar, and that, as his career progressed, plot and character became steadily more important to him. His fools and philosophers remain much the same from *Headlong Hall* to *Gryll Grange*; but after *Headlong Hall* he lavishes progressively greater care on his heroes and heroines—sometimes even to the detriment of his satire—and nowhere is this serious side of his work more evident than in his sensitivity to the plight of the intelligent woman. Beginning with simple mockery of commonplace standards of female education and behavior, he ends by creating women who share equally with men in the dominion of thought and reason.

In her study of women's roles in women's novels, Hazel Mews observes, "If Englishwomen up to the end of the eighteenth century did not know their place or understand their role it was not through want of a sermon to point it out or a conduct book to reiterate the instructions that were preached from the pulpit."[5] A sampling of these conduct books, many of them in print well into the nineteenth century, provides an epitome of the attitudes against which Peacock was in revolt.

Typical of the advice extended to young women in Peacock's time was Dr. John Gregory's *A Father's Legacy to His Daughters,* first published in 1774 and still famous as an object of Mary Wollstonecraft's wrath in *A Vindication of the Rights of Women.* Gregory is particularly fond of drawing distinctions between "you" women and "we" men, the latter being subjects of strong passions, hard hearts, and dissolute manners. But women, he observes, are different: "Your superior delicacy, your modesty, and the usual severity of your education, preserve you, in a great measure, from any temptation to those vices to which we are most subjected. The natural softness and sensibility of your dispositions particularly fit you for the practice of those duties where the heart is most concerned."[6] Gregory goes on to advise his daughters that "one of the chief beauties in a female character, is that modest reserve, that retiring delicacy, which avoids the public eye, and is disconcerted even at the gaze of admiration." He warns that "wit is the most dangerous talent you can possess," and that although "wit is perfectly consistent with softness and delicacy, yet they are seldom found united." Nor should women presume to equality by "conversing with us with the same unreserved freedom as we do with each other," a proscription which would surely have amused Lady Clarinda of *Crotchet Castle.*

Gregory is especially preoccupied with "delicacy," perhaps the period's most widely used term of approbation for female behavior. For Gregory the term extends to physical activity as well as to conduct. He advises exercise in moderation, but he counsels, "We so naturally associate the idea of female softness and delicacy with a correspondent delicacy of constitution that when a woman speaks of her great strength, her extraordinary appetite, her ability to bear excessive fatigue, we recoil at the description in a way she is little aware of." Peacock's Maid Marian, the equal of any man with a crossbow, would doubtless have been chagrined.

Gregory assigns woman a passive role in courtship, though he allows that she should take adequate steps to determine the intended's "character for sense, his morals, his temper, fortune, and family." He provides ways of discouraging unwanted lovers, but he offers no support for the woman who must plead her own case to a reluctant male, nature having "wisely and benevolently assigned a greater flexibility of taste on this subject" to women. He would certainly have censured Morgana of *Gryll Grange* for proposing to the procrastinating Mr. Falconer.

Attitudes similar to Gregory's are found in Thomas Gisborne's *An Inquiry into the Duties of the Female Sex* (1797), a work influential enough to have reached Jane Austen's eyes. Gisborne dilates on female "accomplishments," the term which comprises much of what passes for female education in the period. He allows woman to be trained in dancing, music, and language, not for "display" but to "supply her hours of leisure with innocent and amusing occupations; occupations which may prevent langour and the snares of idleness, render home attractive, [and] refresh the wearied faculties."[7] Like many of his fellow preceptors Gisborne proscribes the reading of romances, a restriction also dear to the heart of Mrs. Hester Chapone. In her *Letters on the Improvement of the Mind, Addressed to a Young Lady* (1773) Mrs. Chapone advises women to read novels and romances only after the most careful selection, avoiding especially the

sentimental kinds of literature; for, as she says, "I am persuaded, that
the indiscriminate reading of such kinds of books corrupts more
female hearts than any other cause whatsoever."[8] She allows the learning of French so that a woman can discuss the "agreeable books of female literature" written in that language, and she adds that Italian is
permissible if one has "leisure and opportunity." But she advises
women to avoid the learned languages, since "the labour and time
they require are generally incompatible with our natures and proper
employments."

As the many songs in his novels attest, Peacock was no foe of musi-
cal education for women, nor would he have denied that fashionable
romances were not worth the reading—by either sex. His refreshing
departure comes in allowing women complete access to the world of
the intellect, where they are free to form their own opinions and to assert those opinions without authorial censure, even in the presence of
men.

One more assessment of the female mind is worth noting, that of
John Bowdler, an edition of whose "Thoughts on the Proposed Improvement of Female Education" appeared within a year of the
writing of *Melincourt*. Bowdler claims to take a middle course between those who hold that women are by nature ignorant and foolish
and may as well remain so and those who argue that "the present state
of female knowledge is below the just level."[9] The first group are
fools, he feels; female education in 1816 is quite adequate to the needs
of men and the requirements of society, needing no "improvements"
to bring it into line with that of men. Patronizingly he subscribes to in-
nate differences in intelligence: "Women are not profound scholars
and philosophers," he notes, "but there is one sort of philosophy
which they understand more practically, and more deeply too, than
any of us. I mean the philosophy of the human heart." Like many of
his coevals he finds higher sanction for his beliefs: "It is plain too,
from the constitution of nature and the declaration of God, that
women are subjected to some authority; an attempt, therefore, to
push them into an undue eminence, can only issue in general
wretchedness."

Such thinking gives credence to Anthelia Melincourt's observation,
noted above, on man's presumed "legitimate and divine right over the
dominion of thought and reason." Her lover, Mr. Forester, captures
her heart when he compares such ideas on women's abilities to those
of "a gardener who should plant a plot of ground with merely orna-

mental flowers, and then pass sentence on the soil for not bearing substantial fruit." He continues:

If women are treated only as pretty dolls, and dressed in all the fripperies of irrational education; if the vanity of personal adornment and superficial accomplishments be made from their earliest years to suppress all mental aspirations, and to supersede all thoughts of intellectual beauty, is it to be inferred that they are incapable of better things?   (188)

Because fashionable beliefs fatuously expressed were always grist for Peacock's satiric mills, it comes as no surprise that he should attack the priggishness of self-appointed advisers to women; what is remarkable is the intensity and consistency of that attack by a so-called laughing philosopher.

Peacock's feminism comprises frontal attacks on the tyranny of arranged marriages and the miseducation of women. The former might be dismissed as a necessary convention of the comic plot; after all, interference in the love lives of the young is a staple in the new-comedy form Peacock adopted for most of his fiction. But the threat of marital unhappiness is everywhere in Peacock, not only in the plots but also, in the earlier novels, in explicit arguments on the subject. The evidence indicates that marriage meddling was more than simply a plot contrivance for Peacock, and as he progressively grants his women an increasing share of the choice of whom—if anyone—they will marry, he accompanies that free choice by greater emancipation in other matters as well.

The self-educated Peacock was no friend of formal education for either man or woman, seeming to agree with his own Dr. Folliot that education leaves people "pretty much as it found them, with this single difference, that it gives a fixed direction to their stupidity" (674). The man who has "finished" his education is a fool, but the victim of "that universal system of superficial education which so studiously depresses the mind of women" (188) engages his sympathy. He clearly sees the damage that undue emphasis on delicacy and accomplishments can do to "that most heavenly of earthly things, an enlightened female mind" (189), and he draws as heroines women who are equal to his men in wit and education and often superior to them in common sense.

Peacock's first novel, *Headlong Hall* (1815), establishes the conversational format for which he is most remembered and the plot device of meddlesome parents he was to use most often in his fiction. The slightly sketched heroines of *Headlong Hall* do little to advance

Peacock's reputation for creating satisfying women, but the book does provide a remarkable closing salvo against arranged marriages.

The conversations in Headlong Hall range over landscape gardening, phrenology, German mysticism, and a host of other Regency enthusiasms. The bulk of the plot is given over to Mr. Escot's capture of the hand of Cephalis Cranium, whose father has promised her to another, richer man "after the manner of the heroic age, in which it was deemed superfluous to consult the opinions and feelings of the lady" (45). Escot's opinions on most subjects are as absurd as those of his fellow philosophers, but he is saved by the fact that he never acts upon those opinions. Chided by his friends over his marrying Cephalis in the face of his own "deteriorationist" philosophy, he offers a particularly strong curtain speech on the state of modern marriage:

> The affection of two congenial spirits, united not by legal bondage and superstitious imposture, but by mutual confidence and reciprocal virtues, is the only counterbalancing consolation in this scene of mischief and misery. But how rarely is this the case according to the present system of marriage! . . . Luxury, despotism, and avarice have so seized and entangled nine hundred and ninety-nine out of every thousand of the human race, that the matrimonial contract . . . is become the most slavish and complicated—a mere question of finance —a system of bargain, and barter, and commerce, and trick, and chicanery, and dissimulation, and fraud. (89)

Such an attitude, voiced after the action has concluded by the most articulate of the characters, indicates that Peacock felt strongly about the matter; furthermore, he was to return often to the unhappiness that could issue from "that most commercial of all bargains, marriage" (108).

Headlong Hall presents some arguments for female emancipation, but it fails to present the women themselves as anything more than objects for the affections of the men. Cephalis and the other young women are "beautiful" and "lovely," and they can sing and dance; but they never enter seriously into the conversations and arguments, nor does Peacock ever show the reader what they think. His next step was to create a woman of intellect who could be mistress of her own life, and that he accomplished in *Melincourt*.

Melincourt was conceived and written during the time of Peacock's closest association with Shelley, who praised the "seriousness" of the book and whose attitudes are frequently apparent in its arguments. Most later readers have shared Van Doren's view that "more than any other of Peacock's novels, *Melincourt* has lost force and appeal with the passage of time."[10] The plot is long and labored, the main characters often prolix and priggish, the conversations lacking Peacock's characteristic wit; on the other hand the arguments are clear, making it possible to see for once where Peacock really stood on marriage and womanhood.

Anthelia Melincourt is introduced as "mistress of herself and of ten thousand a year, and of a very ancient and venerable castle in one of the wildest valleys in Westmoreland" (103). The castle's sublime isolation has not kept a train of suitors from making their way to Anthelia. All have been turned away, however, for Anthelia's theory of love, "being formed by the study of Italian poetry in the bosom of mountain solitude, naturally and necessarily pointed to a visionary model of excellence which it was very little likely the modern world could realize" (107).

Among Melincourt Castle's first guests are the matchmaking Mrs. Pinmoney and her daughter Danaretta Contantina (or "ready money," Peacock notes), whose aim is to marry off Anthelia to one of their relatives. Peacock develops at once the contrast between Anthelia and Danaretta: the former has had her feelings shaped through first-hand association with nature; the latter "had cultivated a great deal of theoretical romance . . . which enabled her to be most liberally sentimental in words, without at all influencing her actions" (108). Danaretta can describe all the theoretical virtues of the man she would marry, but the narrator points out that real virtue would consist only of a "satisfactory certificate from the old lady in Threadneedle Street" (109).

If the Pinmoneys are impossibly crass, Anthelia for her part is impossibly idealistic in describing the man she would marry: "I would require him to be free in all his thoughts, true in all his words, generous in all his actions—ardent in friendship, enthusiastic in love, disinterested in both . . ." (112). The catalogue is long and impressive, and the qualities will be found, as is frequently the case in Peacock, in a man who looks to tradition and classical literature for guidance, Sylvan Forester.

Forester's speeches are just as long-winded as Mr. Escot's, but they lack the deteriorationist's mordant wit; nevertheless, Forester's views on marriage are those of Escot and Peacock, and his criteria for a wife provide a résumé of Anthelia and of Peacock heroines to come. She must be adept in music and poetry, philanthropic, a lover of good books and romantic nature; she need not have money, though it will not be an impediment; her greatest virtue will be a "clear perception of the beauty of truth" (164). Forester touches on Peacock's now-familiar theme when he asks, "What becomes of those ill-assorted unions, which have no basis but money, when, as is very often the case, the money departs, and the persons remain?" (165).

"The harmony of her mind" (163), that essence of womanhood most important to Forester, shows itself from the start in Anthelia's command of music and literature. Dr. Gregory could only have deplored the "unreserved freedom" with which she addresses men, and he would surely have condemned the "dangerous talent" of her wit when she tells Forester that he has "a better opinion of the understandings of women, Sir, than the generality of your lordly sex seems disposed to entertain" (187). That she need not compromise her standards to find a husband in the story does not obscure the fact that she is mistress of herself and not a victim of the "flexibility of taste" which Gregory saw as woman's virtue in the choice of a husband.

Anthelia is the prototype of what Olwen Campbell has called "those women of cultivated and independent minds whom Peacock seems to have put for the first time into English fiction."[11] Women of her vigor, intellect, and assertiveness figure throughout Peacock's remaining novels, with the exception only of *The Misfortunes of Elphin,* in which the roles of women are minor. Moreover, the later heroines are granted their emancipation without their having to resort to Anthelia's lengthy speeches.

In the year after *Melincourt* Peacock published his best-remembered book, *Nightmare Abbey,* based loosely on the exploits of Shelley and featuring not one but two heroines, both of whom are clever enough to evade the marriage arrangements proposed by their elders and intelligent enough to realize that marriage to the melancholic Scythrop is not for them. Both finally abandon the indecisive Scythrop to his Madeira bottle, a resolution which makes it possible for Peacock to present two equally desirable but radically different women without having to say who was the better bride for Scythrop-Shelley.

The sprightly Marionetta, Scythrop's first love, has the conventional Peacockian virtues of present wit and a sound knowledge of music, demonstrated in her singing and in her ability to relate Scythrop's situation to that of Mozart's Don Giovanni. More interesting in a study of the development of Peacock's feminism is Marionetta's intense and mysterious rival, Celinda Toobad. Celinda is in flight from her father's scheme to marry her to a man of his choosing; ironically she seeks refuge in the ruinous tower to which Scythrop has retreated to mull over the uncertainties of love. Identifying herself as

"Stella," she reveals to Scythrop her feelings about the state of her sex: "I submit not to be an accomplice in my sex's slavery. I am, like yourself, a lover of freedom, and I carry my theory into practice. *They alone are subject to blind authority who have no reliance on their own strength*" (404).[12] That she can quote Mary Wollstonecraft supports the narrator's contention that she has "a highly cultivated and energetic mind, full of impassioned schemes of liberty, and impatience of masculine usurpation" (405). Scythrop, of course, falls immediately in love with her. Unable to decide between the two women, he loses them both, finding out too late that he had been Mr. Toobad's choice for Celinda.

As usual Peacock misses no chance to comment on the tyranny of marriages arranged for financial gain. Marionetta's mother had married an Irish officer, and "the lady's fortune disappeared in the first year; love, by a natural consequence, disappeared in the second; the Irishman himself, by a still more natural consequence, disappeared in the third" (365). Scythrop's father had been "crossed in love; and had offered his hand, from pique, to a lady, who accepted it from interest, and who, in so doing, violently tore asunder the bonds of a tried and youthful attachment" (355). Peacock never asks his women to risk poverty, but he is always firmly on the side of the affections in choosing a husband.

With *Maid Marian* (1822) Peacock delved into Joseph Ritson's collection of legends about Robin Hood, but not surprisingly he chose to build his story around Marian. In Peacock's hands she becomes Matilda-Marian, perhaps the most independent and assertive of all his heroines. Lacking, perhaps, in a knowledge of Italian poetry and in graceful conversation, she is nonetheless intelligent enough, "having, in all opposite proposings, sense to understand, judgement to weigh, discretion to choose, firmness to undertake, diligence to conduct, perseverence to accomplish, and resolution to maintain" (450). Of "delicacy" she has little. She excels at the sword and the longbow, though not, Peacock assures us, "like a virago or a hoyden . . . but with such womanly grace and temperate self-command as if those manly graces belonged to her only, and were become for her sake feminine" (451).

Marian's firmness and resolution provide substantial trouble for her autocratic father, who begs, cajoles, and finally rants at her for not giving up the landless Robin Hood. Against his threats to lock her away in his castle, she counters that she will swim the moat, leap from the battlements, or fly through a loophole—actions she seems quite capable of carrying out. At length her father must agree that "she might sometimes be led, but could never be driven" (466), and he finally concedes to Robin the right to lead her to the altar.

With the creation of the rebellious Marian, an equal both physically and mentally of the males in the book, Peacock had reached the limits of his feminism. He never retreated from his championship of the educated and assertive female, but he never again tried a story so completely centered on a female character. In his last two works he returned to country houses and conversations, refining his women from the characters he had already created; nevertheless, they are among his best.

In *Crotchet Castle* (1831) he introduces Lady Clarinda, his wittiest female creation. Like Anthelia she is her own mistress, ready to assert her rights and opinions in the company of men; yet she is preserved from Anthelia's tendency to take herself too seriously. Anthelia's arguments dealt principally with the condition of her sex; but Peacock accords to Clarinda the right to deliver barbs at some of his other favorite targets. Delivering characters of the guests at Squire Crotchet's dinner table, she describes Mr. Wilful Wontsee and Mr. Rumblesack Shantsee (Wordsworth and Southey) as having "turned their vision-seeing faculties into the more profitable channel of espying all sorts of virtues in the high and the mighty, who were able and willing to pay for the discovery" (680). She proves equally adept at defeating her father's schemes to marry her to Crotchet's son, and though she playfully offers to put herself up at auction for whoever can "furnish the commissariat" (669), she ultimately marries the man of her own choice.

Thirty years passed before Peacock published *Gryll Grange.* By that time male British novelists had produced a few Becky Sharps and a host of Amelia Sedleys, though George Meredith had already begun to introduce those women whom Augustus Able found so similar to Peacock's.[13] The heroine of *Gryll Grange,* Morgana, is named for the enchantress in Boiardo's *Orlando Innamorato.* Like Anthelia she has had to resist a train of suitors who do not approach her high standards, but when the right man does appear, Morgana's problem is one of overcoming his inertia. Finally, through the medium of Boiardo's poetry, Morgana proposes to Mr. Falconer. For this "forward" action she is not censured but complimented by the venerable spinster, Miss Ilex, who confesses that "in a case very similar, I did not. It does not follow that I was right. On the contrary, I think you are right; and I was wrong. You have shown true moral courage where it was most needed" (922). In the mellow world of *Gryll Grange* no one will censure Morgana for professing her love, nor will anyone chide Miss Ilex for choosing to remain single.

Peacock's feminism can now be seen as a consistent position held across a long literary career. In *Melincourt* and thereafter, a woman in a Peacock novel may, with her author's full approval, be educated without being considered a bluestocking; she may hold forth in mixed company upon any topic in which she is competent; she may marry the man she chooses, or she may choose to live single. She may ask for advice, but she will finally have to decide all matters for herself; for she owns, in Able's phrase, "no sense of inferiority to any man whatsoever."[14]

Like many of his ideas, Peacock's feminism begins negatively as a reaction to the thinking of his times; but from there it develops into a positive vision of emancipated womanhood, one which demonstrates that interesting female characters were not the exclusive property of female authors. If, as Mario Praz asserts, "all [Peacock] wanted was a type of woman without surprises or profundities, provided she had sweetness, gaiety, and good health,"[15] such women were not the stuff of his fiction.

NOTES

[1]Numbers in parentheses throughout refer to the one-volume edition by David Garnett of *The Novels of Thomas Love Peacock* (London: Rupert Hart-Davis, 1963), the most generally available complete collection of the novels. The author wishes to thank the State University of New York Research Foundation for a grant in support of this study.

[2]Walter Allen, *The English Novel* (New York: Dutton, 1954), p. 152.

[3]*Anatomy of Criticism* (1957; rpt. New York: Atheneum, 1966), p. 309.

[4]*Anatomy*, p. 309.

[5]*Frail Vessels* (London: Athlone Press, 1969), p. 10.

[6]Quotations from Gregory are from a reprint in *Literary Miscellany*, III (London, 1800).

[7]*An Inquiry into the Duties of the Female Sex,* 2nd ed. (London: T. Cadell and W. Davies, 1797), p. 80.

[8]*Letters on the Improvement of the Mind* (1773; rpt. Boston: Leonard C. Bowles, 1822), pp. 144ff.

[9]*Select Pieces* (London: G. Davidson, 1816), pp. 91ff.

[10]Carl Van Doren, *Life of Thomas Love Peacock* (London: Dent, 1911), p. 95.

[11]Olwen Campbell, *Thomas Love Peacock* (London: Arthur Barker, 1953), p. 43.

[12]The last sentence is quoted from *A Vindication of the Rights of Woman* (1792; rpt. New York: Norton, 1967), p. 159. The italics are Peacock's.

[13]Augustus Henry Able, III, *George Meredith and Thomas Love Peacock: A Study in Literary Influence* (1933; rpt. New York: Phaeton, 1970), *passim*.
[14]*George Meredith and Thomas Love Peacock,* p. 88.
[15]*The Hero in Eclipse,* trans. Angus Davidson (1956; rpt. London: Oxford Univ. Press, 1969), p. 89.

State University of New York at Geneseo

ANTONY H. HARRISON

THE AESTHETICS OF ANDROGYNY
IN SWINBURNE'S EARLY POETRY

Death and the achievement of organic continuity with the universe represent the end and culmination of sexual passion for the major figures in most of Swinburne's early poems. Yet it is the enduring *condition* of passion that provides the poet himself with his richest materials,

> For love awake or love asleep
> Ends in a laugh, a dream, a kiss,
> A song like this.[1]

During his most productive years Swinburne undertook to characterize all conditions of passion and its concomitant suffering in men and women of all conceivable states of sexuality—from the noble masculinity of Tristram and Mary Stuart's courtier Chastelard, to Sappho's lesbian strivings for domination and penetration, to the perverse and "feminine" gentleness of the persona in "The Leper." Love is Swinburne's constant subject from his undergraduate lyrics of 1857 to his epic *tour de force, Tristram of Lyonesse,* published twenty-five years later. The diversity of his poems of passion and the complexity of the philosophical precepts which support and dominate them must be recognized in any evaluation of Swinburne's achievement. However, critics have not treated Swinburne's metaphysic of love with the seriousness it demands, and they have only begun to investigate the relationship between the philosophical and aesthetic principles central to his most important poems.[2] Crucial to that relationship is Swinburne's recurrent exploration of androgynous aspects of human sexuality.

Frequently Swinburne's males possess what are normally considered feminine traits, and his women have male characteristics. But

87

sexual ambiguities in his works, though apparent most often in sadistic females with masochistic male counterparts, extend beyond the mere reversal of roles. Mario Praz observes Swinburne's preoccupation with equivocal sexuality in noting the kinship between Moreau's painting *Necessity of Riches* and Swinburne's unfinished novel, *Lesbia Brandon*:

Moreau's figures are ambiguous; it is hardly possible to distinguish at the first glance which of two lovers is the man, which the woman; all his characters are linked by subtle bonds of relationship, as in Swinburne's *Lesbia Brandon;* lovers look as though they were related, as though they were lovers, men have the faces of virgins, virgins the faces of youths; the symbols of Good and Evil are entwined and equivocally confused. There is no contrast between ages, sexes, or types: the underlying meaning of this painting is incest, its most exalted figure the Androgyne, its final word is sterility.[3]

Similarly, Richard Mathews notes Swinburne's fascination with the hermaphroditic iconography of his friend Simion Solomon's paintings, which were "greatly occupied with this ideal of male-female conjunction. . . . Swinburne was intrigued by this aspect of Solomon's art: 'In almost all of these [paintings] there is the same profound suggestion of . . . the identity of contraries.' The union of male and female is paralleled by the possibility of the marriage of all opposites —fire and water, good and evil, Heaven and Hell, high and low."[4]

One should add to this list the marriage of body and spirit. Indeed, the key to understanding Swinburne's apparent equivocation between the mystical spiritualism of what he considered his most important philosophical lyric, "Hertha,"[5] and his continual emphasis on the need for purely physical gratifications of passion, resides in his acceptance of a crucial Blakean doctrine. In his essay on Blake Swinburne explains,

Those who argue against the reality of the meaner forms of "spiritualism" in disembodied life, on the ground apparently that whatever is not of the patent tangible flesh must be of high imperishable importance, are merely acting on the old ascetic assumption that the body is of its nature base and the soul of its nature noble, and that between the two there is a great gulf fixed, neither to be bridged over nor filled up. Blake, as a mystic of the higher and subtler kind, would have denied this superior separate vitality of the spirit; but far from inferring thence that the soul must expire with the body, would have maintained that the essence of the body must survive with the essence of the soul.[6]

Swinburne more clearly defines the nature of man's sublime "essence" in "Hertha," which characterizes the unitary, informing principle of all creation: "before God was, I am," Hertha asserts (II, 72). In this poem Swinburne attempts a reconciliation of all dualities, including sexual duality, which is the fundamental concern underlying his poems about passion: "Out of me man and woman," Hertha declares (II, 72).

These poems suggest that Swinburne imagined a primordial sexlessness in man which precluded the strife of passions men now suffer. This ideal of the "perfect spiritual hermaphrodite" can be seen, like Yeats's Byzantine spirits, as a mystical vision of the prelapsarian harmony of soul which characterized man before incarnation, or as the asexual organicism to which he returns after death. The androgynous ideal for Swinburne reflects the pure, eternal, "Herthian" potential of the soul beyond its temporary embodiment in the mired complexities of blood. As Swinburne remarks of Blake's conception of the eternal androgyne, that being is "male and female, who from of old was neither female nor male, but perfect man without division of flesh, until the setting of sex against sex by the malignity of animal creation."[7] Ironically, the sexual yearning for total physical integration with the beloved object, characteristic of Swinburne's personae, can be seen as an attempt both to escape the torture of insatiable passion and to regain this sexless ideal.

Swinburne was hardly alone in his hermaphroditic quest. As A.J.L. Busst has demonstrated, the figure of the androgyne permeates nineteenth-century literature.[8] In addition, Busst notes that C.G. Jung has powerfully reinforced a major intuition of those writers of the period now considered decadent: "that the androgyne is an archetype of the collective unconscious, that the human psyche is itself androgynous."[9] When dealing with androgynous figures, Swinburne was aware that he was working in a tradition, one that retained unlimited potential for artistic development.[10] Indeed, he seems to have perceived both the optimistic and pessimistic extremes intrinsic to the concept of androgyny that Busst has outlined. On the one hand, androgynous propensities in such figures as the speaker of "The Triumph of Time," Chastelard, Sappho in "Anactoria," and Meleager in *Atalanta in Calydon* reflect an ultimately positive yearning for completion and the sort of continuity with the world which necessitates dissolution of consciousness and quintessential union with the sexless and mystical source of all generation. Although the character of their suffering is largely the subject of the poems they appear in, these figures demonstrate a strength in the resignation to their destiny which borders on optimism and certainly mitigates the pathos we feel for them. This is especially true of Chastelard, for instance, who feels "a kindling beyond death / Of some new joys," and of Sappho at the end of her monologue when she at last perceives how her kinship with nature will immortalize her. On the other hand, androgyny, when conceived of in *purely physical* terms, results in the unbearable intensification of insatiable sexual passions that "shall not be assuaged till death be dead." This pessimistic view of androgyny is developed in "Hermaphroditus," although it also complicates the depiction of figures like Phaedra, Sappho, and Mary Stuart, the heroine of Swinburne's remarkable trilogy of closet dramas. All three are sadistic women whose masculine attributes thrust them into a limbo of vain desires. Most often the optimistic and pessimistic possibilities of androgyny merge for Swinburne when a figure—like Rosamond, Sappho, or Tannhäuser in "Laus Veneris"—does not immediately perceive death as the destined and only complete gratification of his or her passions, as Meleager and Chastelard, for instance, unequivocally do.

The relationship of Swinburne's cast of usually sadomasochistic figures to the symbol of the androgyne is often further complicated by the issue of morality. Questions of good and evil dominate poems like "Laus Veneris," "Dolores," and *Atalanta in Calydon,* while they are important motifs in *Rosamond, Chastelard, Lesbia Brandon, Love's Cross-Currents,* and *Tristram of Lyonesse.* The questions of morality that result from insatiable desires and perverse indulgences arise primarily because passion is dramatized by Swinburne in a rigid pagan or Christian, rather than visionary Blakean, context. Both the constricting hostility of religious or social forces and the physical limitations of sexual indulgence are responsible for the intense frustration that Swinburne's characters suffer. At the same time, the relationship of sadism and masochism to a concept of androgyny is a logical one. As Busst observes, in nineteenth-century literature the figure of the hermaphrodite commonly symbolized sadism and masochism. Although there is nothing androgynous about a *male* sadist or a *female* masochist,

a sadistic woman, in as far as she dominates her male victim, may be considered virile, since she exhibits strength, a male characteristic; and her ability to indulge in her vice depends to a large extent on the male's abdication of his own virility, his masochistic willingness to be ruled—even tormented—by the female[,] showing a weakness of character generally associated with effeminacy. His refusal to assert himself often indicates awareness of the vanity of all action, which must accompany loss of convictions in a world without values, where good is often indistinguishable from evil. It is therefore not surprising that male masochism and its necessary counterpart, female sadism, should be associated so frequently with the attitude of despair and disillusionment reflected in the pessimistic symbol of the androgyne.[11]

While, for instance, Tannhäuser accepts external standards of good and evil and his own consequent damnation, the speaker in "Dolores" rejects the world's standards. Both, however, are deeply affected by accepted morality, whether its effect be manifested in martyred resignation or satanic challenge. Both also quiver under the lash of a burning passion, whose object is represented as a sadistic *femme fatale.* In this light Swinburne's frequent coupling of masochistic males with sadistic women can be seen not at all as perverse indulgence for its own sake, but as a reflection of his intuition that the most deep-seated human sexual yearnings are for a kind of androgynous existence that escapes physical desire, as well as the categories of good and evil, and that returns human energy and essence to its original sexless condition. The artistic result of this intuition is, naturally, either despair or hostility to the world's presiding forces on the part of Swinburne's personae because this ideal cannot be attained by them in life.

Among Swinburne's works, *Atalanta in Calydon* and "Hermaphroditus" most coherently exemplify his respectively positive and negative expressions of the androgynous ideal. *Atalanta,* which made Swinburne an overnight celebrity, has been widely discussed in formal terms as a Greek tragedy; it has been examined as a psychological document; it has been analyzed as a work of consummate poetic skill. I shall explore it, however, as an embodiment of Swinburne's positive vision of androgyny. I shall then discuss the neglected but magnificent brief sonnet sequence "Hermaphroditus," contained in his 1866 volume of *Poems and Ballads,* which very nearly overturned his newly acquired reputation because of its sexual extravagances. This poem is Swinburne's most forceful and poignant representation of the androgyne as a pessimistic symbol.

The titular heroine of *Atalanta in Calydon* is an embodiment of the androgynous ideal, and, significantly, she is nearly bereft of human passions. Atalanta changes "the words of women and the works / For spears and strange men's faces." Although the play's chorus expresses hostility toward her, Meleager perceives Atalanta immediately *as* an ideal and strives to identify with her rather than to copulate with her. Indeed, in *Atalanta* Swinburne's representation of the nature and ends of human passion takes its least physical, most metaphysical form. Early in the poem the chorus perceives love as man's curse and articulates the mythology of Aphrodite's birth and man's concomitant fall into suffering. Beyond this, throughout the play the chorus expands upon Althaea's pessimistic view of the effects of passion:

> But from the light and fiery dreams of love
> Spring heavy sorrows and a sleepless life,
> Visions not dreams, whose lids no charm shall close
> Nor song assuage them waking; and swift death
> Crushes with sterile feet the unripening ear,
> Treads out the timeless vintage.   (IV, 266–67)

Such pessimism culminates in the fourth chorus, which constitutes a hymn of vitriolic defiance to the source of all suffering—including that caused by vain passion—"the supreme evil, God." Yet neither the chorus nor Althaea is able to perceive the spiritual, worshipful quality of Meleager's love for Atalanta:

> Seeing many a wonder and fearful things to men
> I saw not one thing like this one seen here,
> Most fair and fearful, feminine, a god,
> Faultless; whom I that love not, being unlike,
> Fear, and give honour, and choose from all the gods.   (IV, 269)

Meleager is entirely conscious that Atalanta is more divine than human, more ideal than real. Moreover, as Althaea and her brothers are at frequent pains to remind Meleager, Atalanta is by no means conventionally feminine. It makes sense, then, that the yearning for Atalanta that he feels results primarily from a respect for her martial accomplishments and his own aspiration toward the pure and self-contained spirit that he associates with her and with nature:

> My delight, my desire,
>   Is more chaste than the rain,
> More pure than the dewfall, more holy than stars are
>   that live without stain.   (IV, 325)

Atalanta, devotee of Artemis, is continually associated with nature imagery and recognizes her own "forest holiness":

> me the snows
> That face the first o' the morning, and cold hills
> Full of the land-wind and sea-travelling storms
> And many a wandering wing of noisy nights
> That know the thunder and hear the thickening wolves—
> Me the utmost pine and footless frost of woods
> That talk with many winds and gods, the hours
> Re-risen, and white divisions of the dawn,
> Springs thousand-tongued with the intermitting reed
> And streams that murmur of the mother snow—
> Me these allure, and know me.   (IV, 282)

By reputation and self-description, Atalanta, as a huntress and symbol of chastity, becomes almost an extension of the androgynous spirit of nature. Ironically, the figures in *Atalanta* who consider themselves most normal prove to be the least natural. Indeed, in killing the boar, only Atalanta and Meleager show themselves to possess the kinship with natural forces requisite to exert control over them.

Significantly, Meleager is not the first to wound the boar. The best he can do is follow and emulate his ideal. Although he can only approach identification with that ideal in this life, he *can* conceive of a posthumous coalescence with the natural world which Atalanta has come to symbolize. Meleager sees his fate after death as one of reunification, of achieved continuity with the world, analogous to the absorption of vital liquids by organic nature. In lieu of life, the gods will grant him:

> the grace that remains,
> The fair beauty that cleaves
> To the life of the rains in the grasses, the life of the
> dews on the leaves.   (IV, 328)

Thus, although seen by all except Meleager as an unnatural woman, "Virgin, not like the natural flower of things / That grows and bears and brings forth fruit and dies," Atalanta appears to Meleager as perfection, "a god," and "faultless." Despite the fact that his love for her is fatal and fulfills the prophecies of both Althaea and the chorus, his death is ultimately the result of his devotion to an ideal of androgyny. In Meleager's last speech, concerned that the manner of his death will effeminize his reputation, he asks Atalanta to "stretch thyself upon me and touch hands / With hands and lips with lips" (IV, 333). Significantly, he requests only symbolic intercourse. Such an identification with his ideal is all that he aspired to in the tragedy,[12] and, insofar as he achieves this sort of union with her, his respectful passion and his fate become not so much pathetic as noble. His anticipated destiny of a continuity like Sappho's in "Anactoria" with the sexless organic world is the best that can be hoped for in this universe of suffering and strife.

Atalanta may be the only self-sufficient androgyne in this work, but, as Mathews notes, most of the major figures possess both masculine and feminine traits: "Atalanta is armed like a man; Meleager weak-voiced like a woman. Althaea possesses the spirit of a man; Oeneus knows the submission of a woman."[13] Meleager's "effeminate" love for a masculine woman and Althaea's masculine strong will are responsible for all suffering in the play, along with

Oeneus' negligence in worshiping Artemis, the androgynous goddess. That Meleager dies for worshiping Artemis' mortal counterpart is the final irony of the tragedy. Here, as in Swinburne's sadomasochistic lyrics, the corruption of clear divisions between the sexes and the pursuit in carnal reality of an androgynous ideal is the cause of suffering,[14] whether through attempts to merge with the beloved, as in "Phaedra" and *Chastelard,* or to adopt traits properly belonging to the opposite sex. This is not to say that Swinburne rejected the androgynous ideal. On the contrary, Swinburne perceived the inevitably futile compulsion to attain that ideal as the most forceful aspect of human sexuality, at once the source of all passion and the cause of passion's pain. The ideal itself must, however, remain always purely ethereal, intellectual. The androgynous condition represents sexual completion and integrity; it therefore signifies an end to all striving motivated by passion and to all suffering caused by it. The perfected androgyne must be emotionally sterile, dead for the purposes of art. It provides a literary subject only as a counter for characters who are sexually "incomplete" and who exist in a state of perpetual passionate yearning. Atalanta, who is passionless and in every respect sterile, provides such a counter in Swinburne's play. The characters who surround her, however, represent the most sublime material for tragic art, because they strive and suffer tumultuously as a result of their sexual divisions.

Swinburne perceived, as did Gautier, that "it is precisely because [the hermaphrodite] does not truly exist in reality that [it] . . . is so beautiful. 'Rêve de poète et d'artiste,' it is the product of pure art, the 'effort suprême de l'art.'"[15] Swinburne believed that the *idea* of the hermaphrodite "incarnate, literal, or symbolic, is merely beautiful,"[16] and that man's yearning toward the ideal, or a vision of the ideal achieved, constitutes the supreme subject for verse because it combines the ultimate state of passion with the ultimate pathos of suffering. However, the actual physical attainment of the ideal could, paradoxically, produce a monstrous exacerbation of the sufferings induced by human passion. The artistic paradigm for the whole mythology of androgyny thus becomes Swinburne's poem "Hermaphroditus." In *Notes on Poems and Reviews* he acknowledges both the perfection of the hermaphroditic ideal *and* the necessary sterility of any physical achievement of that ideal: "The sad and subtle moral of this myth, which I have desired to indicate in verse, is that perfection once attained on all sides is a thing thenceforward barren of use or fruit; whereas the divided beauty of separate woman and man—a thing inferior and imperfect—can serve all turns of life."[17] Yet, *insofar as* an androgyne can be made to represent the absolute extreme of vain sexual desires, as it does in "Hermaphroditus," it can serve all turns of art; it is "ideal beauty."

Apparently to Swinburne the most forceful aspect of a *purely physical* embodiment of the hermaphroditic ideal was its unnatural-ness. Hermaphroditus, as depicted by the famous statue in the Louvre, possesses the physical characteristics of both sexes but is not sexually neutralized. On the contrary, his sexual desires and suffering are infinitely intensified by his inability in any way to satisfy the pas-sions of either sex. In the myth, Hermaphroditus' refusal to gratify the nymph of Salmacis represents an unnatural act, and he is requited with an equally unnatural fate, one that equivocally incorporates both the nymph's passion and Hermaphroditus' fearful rejection of it. The poet asks, "Is it love or sleep or shadow or light / That lies between thine eyelids and thine eyes?" And he answers, "Yea, love, I see; it is not love but fear. / Nay, sweet, it is not fear but love" (I, 80). In fact, it is both fear and love, as well as a passion so intense that Hermaph-roditus' fire of yearning can be quenched only with an inconceivable extinction:

> Where between sleep and life some brief space is,
> With love like gold bound round about the head,
> Sex to sweet sex with lips and limbs is wed,
> Turning the fruitful feud of hers and his
> To the waste wedlock of a sterile kiss;
> Yet from them something like as fire is shed
> That shall not be assuaged till death be dead.   (I, 79)

Hermaphroditus is suspended physically "between sleep and life," the literal physical embodiment of the immobility dictated by the mythical Hermaphroditus' sexual duality. He exists only to be contemplated. By extension, conceived of as a real being, the hermaphrodite is not merely sexually impotent, but impotent for action in the world. A still birth, he is suspended in a perpetual state of yearning.

In Swinburne's poem the statue becomes the artistic vehicle for ex-pressing the ultimate extreme of passions felt universally and intensely, by generating in the reader an identification with the hermaphroditic condition of insatiable passion. That identification, however, is miti-gated by the self-conscious and highly crafted form of the poem, and it yields after the first sonnet to a mood of intense pathos that is pri-marily purgative.

In the first sonnet of "Hermaphroditus," Swinburne is able to induce in the reader a state of yearning approaching that which the statue projects, but in order to do so, he must, in the last lines of the sonnet, dissolve the possibility for precise meaning to be derived from the language he uses. Ironically, the poet addresses this tragic embodiment of androgyny as a lover would:

> Ah sweet, albeit no love be sweet enough,
>   Choose of two loves and cleave unto the best;
>   Two loves at either blossom of thy breast
> Strive until one be under and one above.
> Their breath is fire upon the amorous air,
>   Fire in thine eyes and where thy lips suspire:
> And whosoever hath seen thee, being so fair,
>   Two things turn all his life and blood to fire;
> A strong desire begot on great despair,
> A great despair cast out by strong desire.   (I, 79)

The last two verses force the viewer (and the reader) to identify with the statue. The rhetorical structure and effect of these lines is that of a paradox. Because of the simple syntactical inversion of the subject and object of the first line in the second, we are left in a momentary state of intellectual suspension parallel to Hermaphroditus' suspension in a purgatory of sexual desires which "shall not be assuaged till death be dead." Here Swinburne manages to dissolve precise meaning and to approach the perfect expression of an ineffably intense state of "desire" which results from the combination of both male and female sexual passions.

"Hermaphroditus" as a poetic creation imitates an art object which in turn imitates an idea—much as does Keats's "Ode on a Grecian Urn," but the significant difference between the two lyrics is that Swinburne's offers no clear resolution to the "problem" of the poem:

> Or wherefore should thy body's blossom blow
> So sweetly, or thine eyelids leave so clear
> Thy gracious eyes that never made a tear—
>   . . . .
> Yea, sweet, I know; I saw in what swift wise
>   Beneath the woman's and the water's kiss
>   Thy moist limbs melted into Salmacis,
> And the large light turned tender in thine eyes,
> And all thy boy's breath softened into sighs;
>   But Love being blind, how should he know of this?   (I, 80-81)

In the poem's last lines, by referring to the myth out of which the pessimistic concept of the androgyne originated and by projecting himself as a kind of aesthetic Tiresias who witnessed the origin of that concept, the lyric voice reaffirms the purely artistic force of the hermaphroditic ideal, its value in the realm of myth and literature. This realm is admittedly removed from life—a thing of barren hours—but nonetheless serves as a gloss on life. In life the passion for complete physical integration with the beloved, as we see it represented in "Anactoria," "Phaedra," *Chastelard,* and *Tristram of Lyonesse,* and as it appears in most of Swinburne's poems of passion, can be consummated only in death and a return to original continuity with the world. But, according to Swinburne, in art it must never be consummated. For the passions which reflect our quintessential yearning for sexual integration provide the richest material for art, both because they are perennial and recognizably potent forces in all of us, and because art remains the only vehicle for adequately expressing and vicariously mitigating those passions by presenting them as objects of contemplation.

For Swinburne passions in art, no matter how earthy, must be ideal passions, "moral passions." He speaks of Shelley's poetry, "where description melts into passion and contemplation takes fire from delight."[18] Ultimately, for Swinburne sensual experience is always secondary and inferior to intellectual experience. In both its pessimistic and optimistic formulations, the ideal of the androgyne for him, as well as for Gautier, Péladan, and the decadents, represents a "withdrawal from practical life."[19] Swinburne's confidence in the value of such an ideal, the supreme value of art, and the necessity for such a withdrawal is reflected in both his art and his life.

NOTES

[1]From "Felise" in *The Poems of Algernon Charles Swinburne,* 6 vols. (London: Chatto & Windus, 1904), I, 188. Hereafter all citations from Swinburne's poems will be incorporated into the text and will indicate the volume and page number of this standard edition.

[2]Some essays which speak to this issue but which collectively constitute only a prolegomenon to its full exploration include: "Swinburne, Sade, and Blake: The Pleasure-Pain Paradox" by Julian Baird, *VP,* 9 (1971), 49-75; "The Content and Meaning of Swinburne's 'Anactoria'" by David A. Cook, *VP,* 9 (1971), 77-93; "'Ave Atque Vale': An Introduction to Swinburne" by Jerome J. McGann, *VP,* 9 (1971), 145-63; "Swinburne and Kali: The Confessional Element in *Atalanta in Calydon*" by F.A.C. Wilson, *VP,* 11 (1973), 215-28; and the articles by Richard Mathews and John O. Jordan cited below. Even one of Swinburne's best critics, Georges Lafourcade, asserts that the poet possessed merely "une simple théorie de l'amour": "de purement instinctif et sensuel, il devient bientôt raisonné et intellectuel. Eclairé par les doctrines du Marquis de Sade, et jusqu'à un certain point poussé par une conviction personnelle, Swinburne découvre dans la nature cette même loi de souffrance universelle et de mort qui lui était apparue dans le mécanisme des passions." *La Jeunesse de Swinburne* (London: Oxford Univ. Press, 1928), II, 431.

[3]*The Romantic Agony* (Cleveland: Meridian Books, 1950), pp. 290-91.

[4]"Heart's Love and Heart's Division: The Quest for Unity in *Atalanta in Calydon*," *VP*, 9 (1971), 42. Although Mathews makes several points that are similar to my own, his are made in a rather different and more narrowly "religious" context. Mathews limits his discussion exclusively to *Atalanta in Calydon*. His focus in that work is on "Love's paradox: . . . a strong and vital bond of unity between characters and gods within the play, [which] is at the same time the foremost cause of their separation and destruction" (37). Moreover, Mathews discusses androgyny (although he never uses the word) only peripherally, as one of the many "divisions" or irreconcilable opposites that confront the major characters of the play in nearly every sphere of life. He is concerned primarily with the quest in *Atalanta* for a body-soul unity, a generalized "unity of being"—not with a specifically sexual ideal that is passionately sought yet unattainable, and therefore a powerful inspiration for art.

[5]Cf. *The Swinburne Letters,* ed. Cecil Y. Lang, 6 vols. (New Haven: Yale Univ. Press, 1959–62), III, 15.

[6]*The Complete Works of Algernon Charles Swinburne,* ed. Edmund Gosse and Thomas J. Wise (London: Heinemann, 1925–27), XVI, 141–42.

[7]*Works,* XVI, 72.

[8]"The Image of the Androgyne in the Nineteenth Century" in *Romantic Mythologies,* ed. Ian Fletcher (London: Routledge and Kegan Paul, 1967), pp. 1–95. Those writers fascinated by androgyny, if we are to believe Norman O. Brown, possessed an intuition of the universal and profound deeps of human sexual motivation: "The 'magical' body which the poet [Valéry] seeks is the 'subtle' or 'spiritual' or 'translucent' body of occidental mysticism, and the 'diamond' body of oriental mysticism, and in psychoanalysis, the polymorphously perverse body of childhood. Thus, for example, psychoanalysis declares the fundamentally bisexual character of human nature; Boehme insists on the androgynous character of human perfection; Taoist mysticism invokes feminine passivity to counteract masculine aggressivity; and Rilke's poetic quest is a quest for a hermaphroditic body." *Life Against Death: The Psychoanalytical Meaning of History* (Middletown: Wesleyan Univ. Press, Conn., 1959), p. 313.

[9]Busst, p. 6.

[10]In *Notes on Poems and Reviews,* speaking of the Louvre's statue of Hermaphroditus, Swinburne remarks: "It is incredible that the meanest of men should derive from it any other than the sense of high and grateful pleasure. Odour and colour and music are not more tender or more pure. How favourite and frequent a vision among the Greeks was this of the union of the sexes in one body of perfect beauty, none need be told. . . . I am not the first who has translated into written verse this sculptured poem." The best edition of this essay appears in Clyde K. Hyder's *Swinburne Replies* (Syracuse: Syracuse Univ. Press, 1966). This passage is on p. 28.

[11]Busst, p. 56.

[12]John O. Jordan, although emphasizing the oedipal aspect of Meleager's relationship with Althaea and Atalanta's role as a mother substitute, lends support to my argument. He also sees Atalanta as a "strangely androgynous figure," and he suggests that "Meleager and Atalanta are two halves of a single self. His love for her is more narcissistic than, in any literal sense, homosexual, in that she represents an idealized version of himself, a model of what he might have become. Her prowess and bravery in the hunt mirror his own heroic accomplishments. At once chaste and courageous, she embodies precisely that dedication to 'divine deeds and abstinence divine' which Althaea

had urged Meleager to pursue. His plea that she stretch herself upon his dying body and 'touch hands / With hands and lips with lips' (IV, 333) is the expression of a final effort to overcome the tragedy of self-division through romantic love, but such efforts are doomed to failure so long as the differentiation of the sexes persists" (*VP*, 11 [1973], 112). Jordan's general emphasis, however, is on Meleager's contradictory and self-destroying complex of desires to return to and escape from the womb.

[13]Mathews, p. 43.

[14]Although Lafourcade (pp. 384–88) has carefully examined Swinburne's sources for *Atalanta,* he does not note the special ways in which Swinburne adapts Ovid's version of Meleager's tragedy. Ovid does stress Atalanta's equivocal sexuality: "she had features which in a boy would have been called girlish, but in a girl they were like a boy's" (*The Metamorphoses,* tr. Mary M. Innes [London: Penquin Books, 1955], p. 187). Nonetheless, Ovid suggests nothing particularly effeminate in Meleager's character, and he describes nothing unusually masculine in Althaea's. In treating the myth Swinburne clearly saw an opportunity both to suggest the arbitrariness of accepted sexual norms and to stress the enormously complex nature of human sexuality as it relates to the larger metaphysical issues *Atalanta* deals with.

[15]Busst, pp. 41–42.

[16]Hyder, p. 28.

[17]*Ibid.*

[18]*Works,* XV, 127.

[19]Busst, p. 42.

North Carolina State University

HENRY MILLER: YEA-SAYER

When Melville praised Hawthorne for saying "No! in thunder . . . .
For all men who say *yes,* lie,"[1] he spoke for the majority of American
writers from his time to our own. Whether the view be based on a Puritan concept of sin and the distrust of pleasure, the crumbling of
value systems before or after the wars, or on the more current visions
of absurdity, our major tendency has been despairing, self-critical,
and frequently cynical. Not that literature has ever told as much of
pleasure as of pain. But American fiction, in particular, and increasingly so with increasing affluence, has, in novels as various as *Moby
Dick* and *The Great Gatsby,* turned on a soul sickness so severe—
whether in response to cosmic or societal patterns—that the possibility
of warm human responses is practically nonexistent.

While the classic fiction of America is rich with metaphysical and
moral concerns, our failures scream out to us in the literature from its
beginnings, with the world of Huck Finn as deeply flawed as that of
One Flew over the Cuckoo's Nest, where the society is a huge combine
imprisoning and castrating its men. Whether the attack is against
America directly, which is so often the case, or whether the literature
simply springs from the place, it shows a life where little love and delight can occur. Independence and courage continue to be the favored
values, but freedom leads only to frenzied activity and loneliness;
energy results in violence. And the ugly ironies of our racial situation
continue to supply ample material for self-castigation.

The diminutive line of yea-sayers in our classic repertoire—led by
Emerson, Thoreau, and Whitman—petered out after the lush but
often inflated rhetoric of Thomas Wolfe and, as Terry Southern
points out, nearly became extinct with "one last overdose of

schmalz"[2] by such a writer as William Saroyan. But there is one yea-sayer America has yet to meet head-on—Mr. Henry Miller, who be-lieves that the first word a man must write when he finds the "life rhythm, is Yes! Everything he writes thereafter is Yes, Yes, Yes—Yes in a thousand million ways. No dynamo, no matter how huge—not even a dynamo of a hundred million dead souls—can combat one man saying Yes!"[3]

The name Henry Miller has raised many objections, the first and most dramatic being the obscenity charges: this is the man who writes the dirty books. But now that the pornography issue has lost its fire, and the censorship trials of his books are forgotten, perhaps we can see what else Miller says. His obscenity (rather than pornography, if that term refers to literature intended for erotic arousal) cannot shock as it once did, although it may offend some readers enough to drive them away. As Miller lards his writing with crude detail, we recognize the art of the child determined to do what is naughty. And he was very naughty in the thirties.

But Miller was never a man to thrive merely on the act of rebellion or on any masochistic impulse. Nor is he a satirist, whose primary concern is flaw. While he writes convincingly of pain and anger, he is one of the few who also record joyous feelings, in a time when it is not a convention to do so. Critic that he is, Miller is more original in his appreciations and in his honesty in expressing them. *Tropic of Cancer,* his best work, is an incredible song of joy—for freedom to curse, to make love, to eat, drink, beg, and ramble about Paris, unattached. Sadly, for some readers the book's obscenity obscures its real theme, which Miller says is liberty. Whether he is driving across the deserts of America or saying goodnight to a prostitute in Paris, Miller is light-hearted when he feels free. Not since *Walden* has there been such a clear-headed savoring of freedom, which is usually most poignantly shown by those deprived of it.

An important early attack on Miller is in George Orwell's generally appreciative "Inside the Whale." While recognizing Miller as a de-scendant of Whitman in the admirable tradition of acceptance, Orwell maintains, in 1940, that for anyone to say "I accept" is to say that he accepts "concentration camps, rubber truncheons, Hitler, Stalin, bombs . . . and political murders. . . . And on the whole this is Henry Miller's attitude."[4] Orwell was "intrigued" by this man who showed no interest in the Spanish war and wanted only to stay in Paris having a good time. But as the polemicists of the period were to be-come disillusioned in their approach (W.H. Auden, as the most obvious example) and as the taste for propaganda waned, criticism of the apolitical Miller lost its force. And while it was Orwell who made that attack most persuasively, it was he who pointed out a crucial and astonishing aspect of *Tropic of Cancer:* "The thing has become so unusual as to seem almost anomalous, but it is the book of a man who is happy."[5]

Some readers have objected to Miller, the persona of *Tropic of Cancer,* on other ethical grounds. He doesn't care what happens to people, although he may be extravagantly generous at times. Women are so obviously used only for sex that the fact hardly bears mentioning. Always ready to thrive on another's misfortune, Miller rushes out to get the job of the pathetic Peckover, a proofreader, when he is killed in a fall down the elevator shaft. And *Tropic of Cancer* closes on an idyllic note of contentment that comes after a meal he buys with the money his friend asked him to deliver to a girl. If one is looking for an exemplar of Christian virtues, Mr. Miller is clearly not the man to read.

But as one who honestly and refreshingly admits that our joys are not necessarily related to other people or to generous impulses (although we humanitarians may not easily admit the fact), Miller has few equals. He tells of the supreme pleasure that comes from one's own inventiveness—which for the writer will be a solitary exercise. Beginning with the knowledge that freedom and love have never gotten on well together, Miller is one of the few writers who dares to opt for freedom. He is never trapped, as someone like Hemingway was, in an attempt to live up to humanistic values that he does not believe in. Such an attempt fails for Hemingway in *For Whom the Bell Tolls,* for example, where he tries to make romantic and Christian love his themes, while his real instinct is for a violent test of courage for the individual man, an antisocial act. Miller eliminates the possibility of such a problem by stripping away any pretensions to the heroic on the first page of his book. And the poverty and passivity that follow become the luxuries that make freedom possible.

A further objection to Miller's writing is that it is repetitious and boring. Sometimes it is. But that does not negate the inspiring single song of *Tropic of Cancer,* with its opening section like nothing in our literature:

This then? This is not a book. This is libel, slander, defamation of character. This is not a book, in the ordinary sense of the word. No, this is a prolonged insult, a gob of spit in the face of Art, a kick in the pants to God, Man, Destiny, Time, Love, Beauty . . . what you will. I am going to sing for you, a little off key perhaps, but I will sing. I will sing while you croak, I will dance over your dirty corpse. . . .

To sing you must first open your mouth. You must have a pair of lungs, and a little knowledge of music. It is not necessary to have an accordion, or a guitar. The essential thing is to *want* to sing. This then is a song. I am singing.[6]

What clod would be bored by this? And if Miller can free himself of the conventions of the novel as he writes, why shouldn't his readers be as free in their reading, tasting a book wherever and for only as long as they please? Miller wisely advises that "a book should be sought after even if it has only *one* great page in it: we must search for fragments, splinters, toenails, anything that has ore in it, anything that is capable of resuscitating the body and soul" (232). And one page of *Tropic of Cancer* has more exuberance in it than the whole of most other books.

As if these various objections to Henry Miller were not enough to damn him to oblivion, there is one more, which may be the subtlest and the most important of all: his *optimism.* It is simply not fashionable to be an optimist. And the more possessions we have, the easier it is to be glibly pessimistic. From comfortable circumstances we speak with authority of despair—that is, after making the necessary call to the TV repairman. Meanwhile, back in the fiction, we hold American technology and bureaucracy responsible for the death of the soul, considering anyone capable of being happy in this time and place an idiot.

Miller himself is known to some mainly as a critic of America, which is his approach in *The Air-Conditioned Nightmare,* where he repeats the worn attacks we have heard for years. In his unoriginal shouting Miller is not at his best. But what becomes fascinating about this book is the way his natural urge to rejoice prevails, as what begins as a diatribe on America's ugliness and sterility turns into a paean to unusual people and places. In spite of all he finds to attack, and the desire to make that attack, Miller naturally goes from a haughty antagonism to a song of wonder for America's loveliness. The Frenchman J. Rives Childs appreciates, as American critics have failed to do, that this work is to be cherished "not only for his tribute to France but also for his eloquent testimony regarding . . . the South. . . . one of the keenest appreciations of the South ever written and that is saying a great deal."[7] Miller is awed, too, by the American West. The Grand Canyon is "so grandiose, so sublime, so illusory, that when you come upon it for the first time you break down and weep with joy . . . it is one of the few spots on this earth which not only come up to all expectation but surpass it."[8] Out of bleakness Miller discovers the miracles that make a posture of despair untrue for him. And it is this capacity for wonder that shows him at his best.

Miller first rejoices in *Tropic of Cancer* for the act of creation, his writing. In the spirit of Genesis, he contradicts the notion, assumed in the modern period, that the artist's work is agony. "Divine creation, on the other hand, bears no such connotation. We do not think of sweat and tears in connection with the creation of the universe; we think of joy and light, and above all of play."⁹ The theme of artist as sufferer is the focus of Edmund Wilson's well-known *The Wound and the Bow,* which examines the myth of the warrior Philoctetes, who is bitten by a snake on his way to fight and exiled because his wound produces such a horrible smell. Isolated on an island for ten years with the wound that will not heal, he is forced to become reflective, and in doing so he develops superior mental powers. As a result of energies stimulated by his suffering, Philoctetes comes to represent "the conception of superior strength as inseparable from disability."¹⁰ Wilson points out that André Gide, in his *Philoctète,* is even more emphatic on this point, giving an implication "which must occur to the modern reader: the idea that genius and disease, like strength and mutilation, may be inextricably bound up together."¹¹ This concept has become so well established that in this century, with terrifying accuracy, it has been possible to predict the suicides of particular authors; the gruesome trend continues, perpetuating the image of artist as madman and martyr. Miller asks us to contradict this view, suggesting that although "we haven't had any healthy artists for centuries, . . . that's no reason why we can't."¹²

Perhaps Miller's hopefulness for the creator comes from the high-spirited painters he knew in Paris. Always a lover of clowns (he once wanted to be one), Miller was enchanted by the happy and comic creations of these artists:

How grateful I am to have lived with these figures of Seurat. . . . They dwell in sunlight, in a harmony of form and rhythm which is sheer melody. And so with the clowns of Rouault, the angels of Chagall, the ladder and the moon of Miró, his whole menagerie, in fact. So with Max Jacob, who never ceased to be a clown, even after he had found God. In word, in image, in act, all these blessed souls who kept me company have testified to the eternal reality of their vision. Their everyday world will one day become ours. It is ours now, in fact, only we are too improverished to claim it for our own.¹³

Unlike most accounts of the act of writing, which is seen as the painful task of recording rotten truth, Miller sides with the painter for his appreciative art: "Whether you paint flowers, stars, horses or angels you acquire respect and admiration for all the elements which go to make up our universe. You don't call flowers friends and stars enemies, or horses Communists and angels Fascists. You accept them for what they are and you praise God that they are what they are."[14]

Miller loves this world, and Paris is very much the part of it that provides such pleasure in *Tropic of Cancer*. Like the writers of the twenties, he went there to escape; but for him it was more than a retreat where one could hide to write ugly things about America. He revels in an alternative life. For him in Paris, in spring,

> . . . the humblest mortal alive must feel that he dwells in paradise. But it was not only this—it was the intimacy with which his eyes rested upon the scene. It was *his* Paris. A man does not need to be rich, nor even a citizen, to feel this way about Paris. Paris is filled with poor people—the proudest and filthiest lot of beggars that ever walked the earth, it seems to me. And yet they give the illusion of being at home. It is that which distinguishes the Parisian from all other metropolitan souls.   (61)

If the earlier expatriates enjoyed Paris as Miller did, the fiction of the period does not show it. Ironically, it is in the bleak thirties that Henry Miller comes like a wonderful joke, hedonistically proving that life can be fun.

Miller refers to Paris as a whore, which for him is a term of praise. His admiration of prostitutes is not merely for their humanity but because of their rare ability to live without security, to be free. He says of a favorite whore: "She would produce no children, contribute nothing to the welfare of the community, leave no mark upon the world in going. But wherever she went she would make life easier, more attractive, more fragrant. And that is no little thing."[15]

Sex and food are on the same plane in *Tropic of Cancer,* but dinner has the edge. The protagonist is always hungry, always on the prowl for a free meal. "The mere thought of a meal—*another* meal—rejuvenates me. A meal!" (45). Miller acknowledges simply a preoccupation with food—how the idea of dinner keeps an afternoon alive. Although he is extremely hungry, his obsession with the next meal is amusingly normal. And that feast on a crust of bread is no mock heroic venture in this book. Unlike most food in literature, which is there to symbolize fastidiousness or excess, Miller's is real, tasty, life-giving food.

Despite the preoccupation with food and drink in *Tropic of Cancer,* we are spared the lethargy of overindulgence. The protagonist is unusually alert. As unlike Thoreau as Miller is, in obvious respects, *Walden* and *Tropic of Cancer* are similarly awake and clear-headed. *Cancer*'s author might even qualify by Thoreau's standards as the one in a million who is "awake enough for effective intellectual exertion," even, perhaps, as the one in a hundred million awake enough for "a poetic or divine life."[16] A lean and hungry feeling pervades these two remarkable books, which show, as few books have, how a healthy attitude can change the world.

Miller rejoices in his robust physical health, which he equates with a happy mental condition. "Walking along the Champs-Elysées I keep thinking of my really superb health. When I say 'health' I mean optimism, to be truthful. Incurably optimistic!" (45). We so rarely hear anyone mention good health that Miller's account of the normal comes as a pleasant shock. And how quaint it is to meet gratitude.

Miller is ripely along in life by the time of *Tropic of Cancer,* and much of its wisdom springs from that fact. Perhaps like pity and compassion, appreciation is a sensation that comes late to us, only when we have worn out the melancholy ravings of youth and begin to understand that we will die. America's own youth and its preoccupation with the young, so often given as reasons for cultural deficiencies, may well be related to the failure to produce warmth in our literature. Miller agrees that " 'life begins at forty.' For the majority of men it is so, for it is only in middle age that the continuity of life, which death promises, begins to make itself felt and understood."[17] Miller was in his forties when he did his first successful writing, after following the styles of others and working for years at jobs he hated. He was also breaking from marriage, in which he never felt free. Although in *Tropic of Cancer* the protagonist claims to love his wife Mona (as he prowls happily after women in Paris), when she arrives his male freedom is curtailed by female demands, in traditional American fashion. Like the great adventurer Don Quixote, the protagonist of *Tropic of Cancer* must be without a family if he is to be about his creations. For both of these free souls, with maturity comes a tender appreciation for the gifts of food and drink, and one more chance to go down the road.

The most exhilarating discovery in *Tropic of Cancer* is the bliss of life without illusions, a theme Miller sings from the first page: "I have no money, no resources, no hopes. I am the happiest man alive" (1). And with nothing owned or expected, ah, no responsibility either. Acceptance of the world *as is* becomes Miller's key to satisfaction. And if a passive approach does nothing to improve a political or social situation (an aggressive approach is not effective either), Miller believes it *is* the way of individual creativity and the "law of love, which is based on absolute tolerance, the law which suffers or permits things to be as they are. Real love is never perplexed, never qualifies, never rejects, never demands."[18]

The startling thing in Miller is not his subject matter but his attitude toward it. As Orwell notes, his topics are as distasteful as anything in Celine's *Journey to the End of Night,* to which *Tropic of Cancer* has been compared. But the books have little else in common. Miller not only accepts but *embraces* his smelly world, while Celine's spirit is the expected one of disgust. Miller's is a form of Faustian heaven, where being alive is everything. However filthy Paris may be, it is never dead. Its energies, however, are not directed as they would be in America toward achievement and progress. "Over there you think of nothing but becoming President of the United States some day. Potentially every man is Presidential timber. Here it's different. Here every man is potentially a zero. If you become something or somebody it is an accident, a miracle. . . . But it's just because the chances are all against you, just because there is so little hope, that life is sweet over here" (135).

The zero approach, like Miller's attitude toward hunger and freedom generally, suggests a clean and exciting space that allows for life-giving movement. The creator must ensure himself of this freedom by constantly unloading baggage—patients, friends, admirers, possessions —in order to keep himself, as the Chinese say, " 'alive-and-empty.' "[19] While literature often enough attempts to persuade us to abandon our illusions for the sake of truth or self-preservation, Miller's purpose in doing so is that we might love life more. He asks that we change the nature of desire itself: "the monstrous thing is not that men have created roses out of this dung heap, but that, for some reason or other, they should want roses" (88).

In *The Smile at the Foot of the Ladder* Miller allegorizes this concept in a tale about Auguste, the clown, whose job is to lie at the foot of a ladder feigning ecstasy in order to make people laugh. His only delight in the role is the crowd's applause, and he is distraught when he loses the job. Then one night he dreams of falling to earth from a high ladder and landing on the ground as himself. In this he realizes the miracle of being alive and that the potential for joy exists only at the bottom of the ladder. Miller's philosophy of acceptance, "the gift of surrender," is epitomized by the clown, who makes the gesture symbolically. And "it is for us to make it real."[20]

In spite of the plethora of prophets of doom, joyful emotions must hide out in American hearts. Our literature is incomplete and frequently dishonest for so seldom illuminating them. The protagonist of *Tropic of Cancer,* wearied by the conventional pose of despair, proclaims that "everywhere I go people are making a mess of their lives. Everyone has his private tragedy. It's in the blood now—misfortune, ennui, grief, suicide. The atmosphere is saturated with disaster, frustration, futility" (11). Miller's emphasis here is noticeably on what people do to themselves, not on misfortunes that come from outside them. But his urge to accept responsibility for suffering is almost as unfashionable as the suggestion that happiness is possible.

According to Jacques Barzun, the "condition" of despair came into fashion early in the twentieth century and has altered little since then. As a result, writers for a long time have merely imitated an attitude that came about under very different circumstances from their own; they draw from the poison in the air without ever experiencing the particular destruction described. And they never let out the secret that they are sometimes happy. Barzun laments that critics, whose job is to give us new ideas, echo the writers of fiction in their message of hate against the world that has been in vogue for decades now, as they fall into "the dullest of conformities, the conformity of Dissent."[21]

One more reason why literature remains set in its grim track is certainly the mysterious difficulty of making the good dramatic. We expect noble characters to be dull and villains to be vital. In the words of Yeats, "the best lack all conviction, while the worst / Are full of passionate intensity."[22] Dostoevsky struggled to create saints who were dramatic, but Prince Mishkin and Alyosha never succeed as the devilish father Karamazov and the misery-loving Marmeladov do. As Miller says, "the literature of flight, of escape, of a neurosis is so brilliant that it almost makes one doubt the efficacy of health."[23] The subtlety of a quality such as kindness may make it difficult to portray dramatically. But what of the brilliantly fine moments of life, which are as earth-shaking as pain can be? Miller is daring enough to try for them.

American literature's failure to present warm emotions may be irrevocably shaped by the Puritan influence that gave us our first chilling classic, *The Scarlet Letter*. But whether the notion that pleasure is sinful be cause or symptom of a psychological condition, our literature is well established in terms of Freud's unpleasure principle. People often are uncomfortable with happiness. Miller dramatizes this truth in a scene in *Sexus* where a man stands up in a restaurant proclaiming that on his wedding anniversary he is still in love and would like everyone to share his happiness. But instead of joining him in celebration, the other diners refuse to admit what they see. Miller is not first noted for his psychological depth, but he shows considerable insight here into the phenomenon that people lack the honesty and the courage to be happy, and that they are uncomfortable with the happiness of others. Laugh and the world does not laugh with you.

In "The Fate of Pleasure" Lionel Trilling marks the demise of pleasure as a literary subject with the romantic poets of the late eighteenth century. Wordsworth's Preface, with its often-quoted "emotion recollected in tranquillity," also refers to the "grand elementary principle of pleasure," a concept which has been ignored. Trilling suggests that it was with Keats, who showed pleasure at its most sensual level, that the idea of pleasure came into the sincerest doubt. And since then, with our increasing access to luxuries, we have become increasingly suspicious of their effect upon us and so have made "destruction of what is considered the specious good" a standard subject of modern fiction.[24] Presumably the attack is made against the ugliness and dehumanizing qualities of technology, but actually the belief is that the values of pleasure embraced by the bourgeois world hamper our individuality. To yield to pleasure in our time is to consent to the conditional nature of man (and thus not to be free), which is just what Dostoevsky's underground man refused to do, not merely because he envied what society had, which he did, but because he insisted on being unlike everyone else, no matter how disgusting and self-destructive he had to be. It is this factor, suggests Trilling, that puts Dostoevsky, rather than the sunshine-seeking Nietzsche, to whom he is sometimes compared, at the spiritual center of our time.[25]

Some of the prophesies of the yea-saying Miller are eerily coming true. In 1944 he predicted that the East and the West would meet in a "series of deathlike embraces" which would lead to a new coming together with the East. He also foresaw a great emancipation of women, suggesting that the "next great impersonation of the future" would be a woman.[26] His most extreme and optimistic statement is that there would be an "epoch of the threshold," a time in which man and artist would not be separate, and all people would live more creatively.[27]

Miller's most ambitious hopes may never be realized, but they do remind us that civilization does not necessarily decline and that in spite of inhumanity and suffering, now, as always, joy exists. If one of literature's first functions is to record the extraordinary, then the subject of happiness might now be approached as an *unusual* topic. As it becomes more difficult to arouse an audience by demonstrating life's horrors, the writer might startle his readers with the revelation that life is still a miracle. Sometime joy might knock you off your feet. And there may be peace. As Miller says at the end of his great book,

After everything had quietly sifted through my head a great peace came over me. Here, where the river gently winds through the girdle of hills, lies a soil so saturated with the past that however far back the mind roams one can never detach it from its human background. Christ, before my eyes there shimmered such a golden peace that only a neurotic could dream of turning his head away. (286)

It is a stingy lie to hold back praise. Say it. The end is not yet.

NOTES

[1] Herman Melville, Letter "To Nathaniel Hawthorne," in *The Portable Melville*, ed. Jay Leyda (New York: Viking, 1952), p. 428.

[2] "Miller: Only the Beginning," *The Nation* (Nov. 18, 1961), p. 399.

[3] *Tropic of Capricorn* (New York: Grove Press, 1961), p. 290.

[4] *A Collection of Essays* (New York: Harcourt Brace, 1946), p. 218.

[5] *Ibid.*, p. 217.

[6] (New York: Grove Press, 1961), pp. 1–2. Further page references to this edition are included in the text.

[7] "Collecting Henry Miller: or, What Henry Miller Means to Me," in *Collector's Quest: The Correspondence of Henry Miller and J. Rives Childs, 1947–1965*, ed. Richard Clement Wood (Charlottesville: Univ. Press of Virginia, 1968), p. 181.

[8] (New York: New Directions, 1945), p. 240.

[9] Henry Miller, "Of Art and the Future," in *The Henry Miller Reader*, ed. Lawrence Durrell (New York: New Directions, 1959), p. 237.

[10] (New York: Oxford Univ. Press, 1965), p. 235.

[11] *Ibid.*, p. 237.

[12] *Henry Miller: Letters to Anaïs Nin*, ed. Gunther Stuhlmann (New York: Putnam, 1965), p. 190.

[13] *The Smile at the Foot of the Ladder* (New York: New Directions, 1948), pp. 48–49.

[14] *Stand Still Like the Hummingbird* (New York: New Directions, 1962), p. 40.

[15] *Quiet Days in Clichy* (New York: Grove Press, 1965), p. 61.

[16] *Walden* (New York: Random House, 1950), p. 81.

[17] "The Wisdom of the Heart," *The Henry Miller Reader*, p. 259.

[18] *Ibid.*, p. 264.

[19] *Ibid.*, p. 260.

[20] *The Smile at the Foot of the Ladder*, p. 47.

[21] *The Energies of Art* (New York: Harper, 1956), p. 16.

[22] "The Second Coming," *The Collected Poems of W.B. Yeats* (New York: Macmillan, 1965), p. 185.

[23] "The Universe of Death," *The Henry Miller Reader*, p. 206.

[24] *Beyond Culture* (New York: Viking, 1965), p. 76.

[25] *Ibid.*, p. 77.

[26] "Of Art and the Future," pp. 232, 241.

[27] *Ibid.*, p. 232.

Howard University

BOOK REVIEWS

Richard H. Brodhead, *Hawthorne, Melville, and the Novel.* Chicago: Univ. of Chicago Press, 1976. Pp. viii, 216. $11.50; Phoenix paperback reprint, 1977. $4.50.

This study of Hawthorne and Melville necessarily owes much to previous work concerning the nature of fiction and the presence of romance and novelistic elements in American narrative. Genre critics have directed attention to the different kinds of reality that are refracted into fiction; Richard Chase, among others, has defined the romance-novel as a traditional American form; and Northrop Frye (whom Brodhead adduces to clarify his own approach to the subject) has pointed out the existence of "basic fables" in all fiction and has suggested that the degree to which these fables are displaced distinguishes one fictional form from another. Brodhead joins this ongoing dialogue perceptively. He focuses on the five novels written by Hawthorne and Melville between 1850 and 1852—*The Scarlet Letter, Seven Gables, The Blithedale Romance, Moby-Dick,* and *Pierre*—and demonstrates how, at their characteristic best, these two writers adapt distinct "representational modes" to the purposes of their fiction. Intent on telling a story, Hawthorne and Melville nonetheless search out primary forms of romance which thwart "sequential narrative"; the result is the mixed and intensified forms their novels possess.

After setting the terms of his discussion, Brodhead devotes one large section of his study to Hawthorne and one to Melville. In each section, he first explains the manner in which the writer's imagination came to the creating of fiction. He considers at some length the well known passage from Hawthorne's "Custom-House" sketch which evokes the metaphor of the neutral ground, and he takes seriously (as I believe he should) the scorn Hawthorne imagines his ancestors directing at him for being "'A writer of story-books!'" His implication that the term "'story-books'" in this context signifies only *tales* may well be too limited an interpretation: Hawthorne's ancestors would hardly have distinguished between forms of fiction. But Hawthorne, as Brodhead goes on to show, did just that in *Mosses from an Old Manse* when he resolved "at least to produce a novel, that should evolve some deep lesson, and should possess physical substance enough to stand alone." And by the time of "The Custom-House," with a novel completed, he had come (again?) to a point at which "the role of the artist once more seem[ed] valid to him." Out of a concern to stress Hawthorne's developing attraction to larger forms of fiction, Brodhead tends briefly to load the terms of his argument. Since *The Scarlet Letter* was conceived as a tale, since Hawthorne's original plan was to include it along with several other works in a volume entitled "Old-Time Legends: Together with Sketches, Experimental and Ideal," it is hardly fair to see Hawthorne "rejecting the idle story and embracing the novel" in 1850. Nonetheless, Brodhead's account of the imaginative habits Hawthorne brought to, and developed in, his longer fictions is both valuable and persuasive.

In beginning his discussion of Melville, Brodhead defines concisely the expansive tendency of Melville's imagination. Indeed, "The Art of the Diver" is one of the strongest chapters in the book. Brodhead moves from the exuberant metaphors of Melville's letters to the unfolding strategies of his fiction; typically, the language of "each formulation" opens up vistas "that require new formulations." The result is that Melville's "fictional techniques, like the hypotheses in his letters, are both brilliantly adequate and instantly obsolete." Melville, that is to say, adopts fictional forms for the telling of a story (*Mardi* is a classic and extreme example) and then breaks through them because of a need to include visions or questions or meditations those forms cannot accommodate. He explores reality rather than representing it. And because of his conviction that inscrutable mystery lies at the heart of the universe, his effort as a novelist is to merge fictional forms and epistemological concerns—"sufficiently organized," as Brodhead says, to evoke the reality of the mystery that lies beyond the range of linear narrative.

The high quality of Brodhead's treatment of individual novels comes in large part from the manner in which he keeps his thesis in clear focus. With his analysis of the relationship of the public world and the private world in *The Scarlet Letter,* for example, Brodhead is able to demonstrate that Hawthorne puts distinct fictional modes in the service of his artistic vision, thereby achieving an effect of doubleness that pervades the romance. His excellent discussion of *The Blithedale Romance* leads him to confront the problems of revelation that inhere in Miles Coverdale as narrator: "a self-deceiver," he believes, "tells a story about self-deception." The "self-exploring forms" of *Moby-Dick* and *Pierre* offer provocative, albeit diverse, evidence of Melville's struggle with form. Committed to radically different visions of reality, characters such as Ahab and Stubb contribute to the "alternation of portentous romance and comic realism" in *Moby-Dick.* And with regard to *Pierre* Brodhead concludes that Melville, "having set out to use the conventions of the sentimental novel for his own purposes, finds that they have used him." It is a well-earned synoptic statement.

One disconcerting feature of Brodhead's study is his addiction to possessives such as the "novel's form," the "novel's energies," and "fiction's reality." Nine of these possessives greet one on the opening page of the first chapter. It is not simply that such usage lacks grace— though Brodhead's observation that the problem in *Blithedale* arises because "the secret's worth to his [Hawthorne's] book's meaning and to its plot fail to coincide" might well make one fight the battle against awkwardness with renewed vigor. It is primarily that such usage can lead to inaccurate statements. When Brodhead says that "Hawthorne's world is governed by the moonlit room's sense of haunted interconnectedness," he is telling us that the *room* has this haunted sense. He has animated the room and given it a feeling that belongs to Hawthorne. Happily, what Brodhead's study offers overbalances this mischievous stylistic habit. Brodhead has not only joined but advanced the critical dialogue on Hawthorne, Melville, and the novel —and advanced it in significant ways.

Indiana University   TERENCE MARTIN

Kenneth Curry, *Sir Walter Scott's* Edinburgh Annual Register. Knoxville: Univ. of Tennessee Press, 1977. Pp. 217. $13.95.

Professor Kenneth Curry has assembled five of Scott's pieces as well as the pompous but hard-to-come-by Prospectus, which Scott might have helped compose, from *The Edinburgh Annual Register.* He has prefaced the selections, here reprinted for the first time, with an informative and useful introduction treating the political, literary, and commercial aspects of the *Register*'s history. Of special interest is his demonstration of the extent to which both Scott and Southey used the annual histories written for the *Register* in later historical and biographical work.

It is possible, however, that the chief benefit of Curry's efforts is aesthetic. Those wishing to arrive at a proper sense of gratitude to him had best visit the usually obscure corner of their libraries where the *Register* is shelved, take down a volume, preferably one whose inner margins have been devoured at the bindery, and read as much as they care to. It is no discredit to Curry's editorial achievement that our admiration for it is largely based on its attractive format.

What ingratitude might exist would arise from the quality of the pieces themselves. They hardly represent Scott at his best. The essay on contemporary poets shows that Scott was a far better critic of fiction than of poetry (although his opinion of Wordsworth was to change for the better); the "Remarks upon the French Order of Battle" —another piece atoned for later—is an unconvincing attempt to demonstrate that Napoleon's tactics were too "obvious and coarse" to entitle him to the stature of a Frederick the Great; "The Inferno of Altisidora," a comic imitation of Swift and Mackenzie, depicts "Scotch reviewers" as "playing at racket" with new books. It is comparatively brief, and moderately enjoyable, but it could still bear pruning. This leaves two substantial pieces: "On the Present State of Periodical Criticism," with its shrewd observations on the role of self-interest in literary affairs, and the hostile "View of the Changes Proposed and Adapted in the Administration of Justice in Scotland," a polemical anticipation of Malagrowther that contains some of Scott's most revealing, and Burkean, thoughts on the management and mismanagement of institutional reform.

If much of this material is dull, it is also useful. Scott was too important and often too puzzling an author not to require the sort of illumination provided by his occasional writings, particularly when his novels are subject to frequent invasions by the modes of rhetoric represented here. Moreover this particular volume, in its inevitable diversity, serves as a useful reminder that some of the contradictions that puzzle us in the novels have parallels in his periodical efforts and result in part from conflicting roles and attitudes adopted during his lifetime. Scott emerges here as the Tory simultaneously serving a party and deploring partisanship; the adherent of the Union defending the Scottish idiom in law, language, and custom; the military analyst offering precise geometric diagrams to illustrate Frederick's strategy, yet in the same piece exhibiting the equivalent of military anti-intellectualism in his discussion of the Peninsular resistance to the French. Not all of Scott's contradictions arose from reflections on the Jacobites.

A few thistles: It seems inconsistent to imply that Scott later inserted the annual histories of 1814 and 1815 into his *Napoleon* "with little change" (p. 38) and to assert further on that he "quite often rewrote, condensed, added new material, and . . . discarded what he had written" (p. 42). Scott, of course, did both. (The question is not entirely academic, for the earlier histories, partly because of their occasionally surly partisanship, are livelier than the *Napoleon.*) Moreover, Curry at times edits with too light a hand. Not every reader will know that "a certain noble peer" (p. 163) who was savaged by the *Edinburgh Review* was the Earl of Lauderdale and that Brougham was the savager, but every reader will be curious. And Corelli, contrary to Scott, did not compose the "Devil's Concerto" (p. 132); it was Tartini who composed the "Devil's Trill" sonata. Again, the "vapid and extensive" innovations deplored by Scott in the essay on legal reform (p. 183) testify to Curry's accuracy of transcription, but surely "rapid" was first intended.

These carpings notwithstanding, Professor Curry has given us an attractive and helpful book.

San Jose State University   ROBERT C. GORDON

Richard Beale Davis, *Intellectual Life in the Colonial South, 1585–1763.* Knoxville: Univ. of Tennessee Press, 1978. Pp. 1749, 3 vols. $60.00.

Richard Beale Davis is the foremost authority on the colonial literature of the South, and his three-volume *Intellectual Life in the Colonial South, 1585–1763* is the summation and distillation of a lifetime's work. The scope of the book is immense, but Davis's expertise is more than equal to the encyclopedic qualities of the book's multifarious contents. Nothing compares with this book for any other large area or time in American intellectual life. What comes closest is Davis's own earlier work, *Intellectual Life in Jefferson's Virginia 1790–1830* (1964), but it dealt with a more restricted time and place. The organization (topical and chronological) and method (historical and critical) in the two books are similar, but the current three-volume study has some key differences—most notably the clarion call for future students to work in the period. In effect, Davis asks that his own *magnum opus* be superseded—but I do not believe that it ever will be. For the book performs three essential tasks: it summarizes what primary materials exist for the study of colonial Southern intellectual life—and it summarizes the scholarship that exists about these basic materials; secondly, it interprets, often with brilliant insights, the primary materials; and thirdly, it relates the various aspects of intellectual life to one another: art to music to painting to literature to religion to books to gardens to plays to history to maps to education to law to Indians to oratory to ideas to architecture. No one else is likely to attempt such a feat. And no one else would succeed. We can expect numerous later studies to disagree with, and a few to correct, Davis's work. But all later students will begin with Davis. And for the most part, later students will only amplify what Davis has said and publish the manuscripts that he has called our attention to.

Because it is such a dominant book, it invites comparison with the older classics of New England intellectual life, Perry Miller's *The New England Mind: The Seventeenth Century* (1939) and *The New England Mind: From Colony to Province* (1953). These two books, especially the former, are the basic works in the modern study of American Puritanism. They are brilliant, profound, and provocative studies. The example of Miller and of his writings has inspired most of our best colonial scholars of the present generation. The former book presents a monolithic portrait of New England Puritanism. The portrait is not precisely true for any single American puritan of the seventeenth century (although Miller pretended it was for all of them), but it is a fascinating synthesis of New England intellectual history. It is read by all specialists in early American literature, and (in the manner of most classic long works of scholarship) it is cited more frequently than read. But it is a hard book to find very *useful,* for what it attempts and succeeds in doing is to present and describe a paradigm, a structure, a total system that is an interrelated whole. Like Davis's *Intellectual Life in the Colonial South,* Perry Miller's *The New England Mind* is a work of genius. One can read it with admiration and learn constantly from it—but he cannot return to it for information about William Bradford or Thomas Hooker or John Cotton or Increase Mather or anyone else. Although every serious student of colonial American literature and culture must read it once, no one consults it frequently. So too, every serious student of colonial American literature and culture will read Davis's book through once—but everyone who does so will find frequent reason to consult it time and again. If you want information about Captain John Smith or Sir John Randolph or Bacon's Rebellion or music in seventeenth-century Virginia, you'll find it in Davis's *Intellectual Life in the Colonial South*. And at the same time, the book presents a paradigm of the Southern mind. It is now the fundamental work on Southern colonial culture.

The book is divided into ten chapters, all of which are monograph-size in length. All are based on painstaking research, citing manuscripts in half a dozen countries and throughout the States. The first chapter (102 pp., plus 20 pp. of bibliography and notes) is entitled "Promotion, Discovery, and History" and contains separate appreciations of John Smith, Bacon's Rebellion, Robert Beverley, Hugh Jones, and William Stith. Chapter Two (143 pp., plus 38 pp. of bibliography and notes) is devoted to "The Indian as Image and Factor in Southern Colonial Life." I especially admire the organization and overall interpretations of this chapter. It opens with a discussion of the "Southern Anglo-American Literary and Philosophical Concepts of the Red Man." Next Davis considers "The Red Man as His White Neighbor Saw Him," treating individually such topics as "Sports and Games," "Marriage and Burial," and "White Ideas of Red Origins." Then Davis takes up "The Frontier: Its Effects on Red Man and White," and he concludes with a section on "Communication: Practical and Artistic," with details on "The Intermediary: The Interpreter and His Role," "White-Indian Oratory: Formal and Informal," and "The White-Indian Treaty: Politics and Art." Such summary as I am giving necessarily omits the perceptions and the information that occur on every page. Let me give one example of the kind of information and interpretation Davis includes. Since the early 1960s when I first encountered Richard Lewis's poem on Madoc as the earliest European discoverer and settler in America, I have been interested in the Madoc myth and have found a number of evidences of belief in the "Welsh Indians" in Colonial America. I eagerly read the recent accounts of Madoc published by D.B. Quinn, Samuel Eliot Morison, and Richard Deacon, as well as the splendid edition of Jamestown materials, 1606–1609, edited by Philip L. Barbour. But when, I have wondered, did the myth of Welsh Indians (i.e., Indian descendants of Madoc) begin? That it existed in the late seventeenth century I knew. But I had missed the significance of that passage in Peter Wynne's letter of November 26, 1608 (in Barbour, p. 246) where Wynne writes that "the people of Monacon speak a far deffering language from the subjects of Powaton, theyr pronunciation being very like welch so that the

gentlemen in our Company desired me to be theyr Interpretor."
Wynne's implication to his English correspondent (as Davis points out
on p. 174) is that the Monacan Indians spoke a Welsh dialect. Thus
Wynne is indirectly making the first claim to have identified a tribe of
"Welsh Indians" and is providing a kind of evidence for the mythic
Welsh discovery of America. No earlier reader of Wynne's letter had
realized these implications. Davis does not dwell on the point; and the
casual reader might assume that Davis is merely repeating what is
common knowledge; but it is new and—at least to those who care
about such things—extremely significant.

Chapter Three, "Formal Education, Institutional and Individual"
(127 pp., plus 35 pp. of bibliography and notes), completes Volume
One of this magisterial study. Volume Two opens with "Books, Libraries, Readings, and Printing" (137 pp., plus 37 pp. of bibliography
and notes). In addition to separate discussions of the numerous private book collections of a multitude of colonial Southerners, Davis
writes the best account yet published of the reading tastes in colonial
America. Chapter Five, the shortest one (73 pp., plus 24 pp. of bibliography and notes) in the three volumes, concerns "Religion: Established, Evangelical, and Individual," with an interesting section on
"Deism and Rationalism." But Davis only seems to make his section
devoted to religion relatively short, because the following Chapter Six
takes up a related subject: "The Sermon and the Religious Tract" (99
pp., plus 21 pp. of bibliography and notes). Most of the sermons
Davis discusses exist only in manuscript. Not only has no one else read
all of them—no one else knew that so many Southern sermons existed.
It is one of the many absolutely new facts—and fields—revealed by
Davis. Chapter Seven, "Science and Technology, Including Agriculture" (186 pp., plus 39 pp. of bibliography and notes), is primarily organized by subject (e.g., botany, zoology), with valuable notes on the
important scientists. The section on "Agriculture, Theory and Practice" concludes with a fascinating discussion of the "Literature of
Colonial Agrarianism." Included in the "Farm-related Technology"
section are such topics as the brewery of John Mercer and the viticul-
ture of Governor William Berkeley and Robert Beverley.

The final volume opens with Chapter Eight, "The Fine Arts in the
Life of the Southern Colonist" (193 pp., plus 36 pp. of bibliography
and notes). The longest section concerns architecture, with separate
consideration of the kinds of private homes in the different areas.
Other sections of this chapter are devoted to the ornamental garden,
graphic arts, music, and the theater. Chapter Nine deals with "Litera-

ture, Principally Belletristic" (200 pp., plus 32 pp. of bibliography and notes). It is a splendid survey of Southern colonial writing. All major and minor writers are discussed, the humor appreciatively noted, and their various degrees of self-consciousness as Americans perceptively evaluated. The final Chapter Ten investigates "The Public Mind, Politics and Economics, Law and Oratory" (124 pp., plus 22 pp. of bibliography and notes). Much attention has been paid by other scholars to politics and economics and, to a lesser degree, to law. But no one before Davis has evaluated the great mass of oratory that exists in the colonial assemblies and in the colonial legal records. The courts and assemblies were the primary training ground for the writers and orators of the Revolution. Once again Davis delineates an enormous field and first sets forth its contents and boundaries. The book concludes with an epilogue characterizing the Southern colonial mind and demonstrating its influence upon later traditions of the nineteenth- and twentieth-century South.

Davis's *Intellectual Life in the Colonial South, 1585–1763* is a magnificent achievement. I predict that it will, in the next several decades, come to be regarded as the pivotal book in the history of Southern colonial studies. Until now, studies of Southern colonial culture have been few and partial. But it will spawn a rich progeny. By his numerous specialized articles and by his several splendid books in the field of Southern colonial studies, Davis has not only created a large scholarly field, he has also furnished a model for future students of colonial Southern culture to emulate. All future students of various aspects of intellectual life in the colonial South will be indebted to Davis, and many of these students will emulate his model.

University of Delaware   J.A. LEO LEMAY

John H. Fisher, ed., *The Complete Poetry and Prose of Geoffrey Chaucer.* New York, London: Holt, 1977. Pp. xiii, 1032. $12.50.

This latest edition of Chaucer's works is much to be welcomed for its completeness of text, and for the reliable, balanced, helpful apparatus. Such a massive achievement contained in over a thousand well-filled pages is not to be summed up in a brief review. The edition must be tested by readers and teachers for some years. As a preliminary assessment I should expect it to be a very strong candidate for the position of chief teaching textbook of Chaucer's works in the United States. That is its obvious and proper intention. It does not seem so likely to displace Robinson's work as the dominant general scholarly edition.

The book is well designed. Each text is accompanied by a commentary, including glossed words and a few textual notes, at the foot of the page. Each work, and each section of *The Canterbury Tales,* is prefaced by a short essay of introduction, and at the end of the texts are sections on the "place of Chaucer" in English culture, "Chaucer in his Time," "Chaucer's Language and Versification," "The Text of this Edition," and a Bibliography. There are five interesting plates (the Hoccleve portrait and some manuscripts). An important new feature is the inclusion of the *Equatorie of the Planets* [*sic*]. As far as spot tests can show, the book is remarkably free from misprints as a whole, though p. 565 is unlucky with two.

It is natural that the introductions should not always command assent, but they are very brief, fair, and on the whole representative of modern scholarship. They rightly attempt little in the way of literary criticism. The important new date of 1368 for *The Book of the Duchess* is registered, though oddly enough with no reference anywhere that I could find to its discoverer, Professor J.N. Palmer in *Chaucer Review* 8 (1974), pp. 253–61. In general there is no attribution of views to their originators except in rare instances, as to Professor D.W. Robertson, who is several times mentioned. Apart from this there is a rather arbitrary selection of references, and there seems no reason, for example, at this late date, to give further advertisement to Margaret Galway's old biographical fantasies. There is more historical assumption of historical reference in Chaucer's work than can always be justified. Of more literary importance is the resurrection of the nineteenth-century view that *The Parliament of Fowls* was written before *The House of Fame,* and that each is tied to a royal occasion. The evidence is not suggested, while on the other hand the error about 'king Scipion' in *The Book of the Duchess,* which is repeated in *The House of Fame,* is noted as corrected in the allegedly earlier *Parliament of Fowls.*

The text is accompanied by a running commentary. Here one may compare Professor Fisher's edition with those of his natural rivals, Professors Baugh, Cawley, and Pratt. I have made a spot check based arbitrarily on Baugh's edition *Chaucer's Major Poetry* (1963), p. 152, "General Prologue" 1(A) ll.152–93, whose format is very similar to Professor Fisher's edition. Fisher gets a remarkable 52 lines, in a comparable page, to Baugh's 42 and Pratt's 39. Both Fisher and Baugh make 38 glosses or brief comments, to Pratt's 42 glosses. It is interesting to see what these various scholars do and do not consider needs glossing or explaining. Baugh and Fisher both gloss, and Pratt and Cawley do not gloss, *smal coral* (158), *a fissh that is waterlees* (180). Baugh glosses, but Fisher, Pratt and Cawley do not gloss, *heng* (160) *Another Nonne* (163) *that text* (177). Only Pratt, of the four, glosses *therto* (153), *spanne* (155), *bar* (158), and only Pratt and Fisher, the most recent and emancipated, add the meaning of "sexual pleasure" to *venerie* (166). (Fisher is best of the four on Chaucer's puns.) I refrain from further detail. To sum up, although all editors vary unpredictably, Fisher gives less elementary information than Pratt, and slightly more annotation than Baugh, though none of Baugh's references to modern studies. Fisher has regrettably no backing-up glossary at the end of the book, where Baugh is strong. Baugh's edition is not complete, while Pratt and Cawley contain only *The Canterbury Tales*. Fisher scores strongly in the nature of his commentary, for an audience of relative beginners, and in his completeness, and may be considered the best so far, but he is philologically less helpful than Baugh.

Fisher's text of *The Canterbury Tales* sensibly follows the Ellesmere order, as in Robinson. He has reconsidered the actual texts of all the poems, where again I have only taken samples. He discusses his principles very frankly. As is usual and probably desirable for the market envisaged, capitalization, punctuation, usage of i/j, u/v, etc., are modernized. Treatment of final *-e* is "conservative" though with some "inevitable" modernization, and "filler words" needed or not needed for scansion are "sometimes included or omitted in the light of the manuscript tradition, sometimes causing defective but still rhythmic lines" (p. 966). There is opportunity for inconsistency and confusion here, especially since Professor Fisher on page 963 comes out firmly (and rightly) for Chaucer's use of the "iambic pentameter." To take but one example; in *The Book of the Duchess* 1.33, where the only authority is Thynne's text, *trewly* is emended to *trewely*; 1.34 *tel to telle*; both following Koch. The emendations improve the meter, and I applaud them. Why then retain the unmetrical *sterles* in *Troylus* I, 416, since *Troilus* is metrically pretty regular? And then again in *The Parliament of Fowls* 1.15 *and* is inserted into the copy-text, and *of* in 1.29 (neither insertion noted), obviously for the meter, and in each case wrongly, since there is a final *-e* to be sounded in each line; while 1.33 hobbles painfully because *theryn* is deprived of its final *-e*. *The Parliament of Fowls* comes off unluckily in the first few stanzas, since the textual note to 1.2 is wrong—it states the opposite of the case—and the gloss to *can* in 1.14 as *can* rather than *know* is doubtful.

So far as a general impression goes the text of *The Canterbury Tales* is fairly near to Robinson, though with enough variation to show that it has been independently considered. It is based on Ellesmere, with a few interesting variants shown. In general, therefore, the text of all the works may be regarded as reasonable, but is considerably edited, not always consistently.

At the end of the book come the explanatory sections already noted which sustain the general standard. The account of Chaucer's life is useful, though disproportionate space is given to the baseless speculation that Chaucer's wife was, like (and at the same time as) her sister, John of Gaunt's mistress. The bibliography concentrates on the period 1964–74, with a few later works and selection of earlier ones. It is admirably subdivided for the less experienced student.

A similar remark may sum up the edition as a whole. It will serve undergraduate students very well, and helps to make Chaucer accessible without cheapening his work. The editor's pleasure in his author comes through very unaffectedly and agreeably—no small tribute, considering the great labor that must have gone into the edition, to both poet and editor.

Emmanuel College, Cambridge   DEREK BREWER

K.M. Elisabeth Murray (preface by R.W. Burchfield), *Caught in the Web of Words: James A.H. Murray and the Oxford English Dictionary.* New Haven and London: Yale Univ. Press, 1977. Pp. 386. $15.00.

Sir James A.H. Murray, schoolmaster and lexicographer, stands at the pinnacle of an ancient tradition. The pedagogic instinct is, perhaps, primarily responsible for the composition of the interlinear English glosses that appear throughout the Middle Ages from the Anglo-Saxon period onward. For example, such glosses as Alexander Neckham's *De Nominibus Utensilium* (ca. 1200); the early English-Latin vocabularies, the earliest of which is the *Promptorium Parvulorum, sive Clericorum* (ca. 1440) with its 12,000 English entries; the earliest Latin-English glossary, the *Medulla Grammatice* (ca. 1460); were all very useful pedagogic tools for the education of young clergy. The *Hortus Vocabulorum* printed by Wynkyn de Worde in 1500 is yet another example of the Latin-English dictionary. This volume, although popular in the early decades of the 16th century, was soon eclipsed by Sir Thomas Elyot's *Dictionary* (1538), known in the later editions as the *Bibliotheca Eliotae.* Elyot's composition was soon incorporated into the larger work of Reverend Thomas Cooper and published as the *Thesaurus Linguae Romanae et Britannicae* in 1565. Bilingual vocabularies and dictionaries continue to appear throughout the 16th century—John Palsgrave's *Lesclarcissement de la langue francoyse* (1530), William Thomas' Italian-English dictionary of 1567, John Florio's Italian-English *Worlde of Wordes* (1598), and Claudius Hollyband's *A Dictionarie French and English* (1593), to name some of the more prominent examples from the period. Despite their lack of immediate ancestry, these English-Latin glosses and bilingual dictionaries from the 13th century through the 16th are all seminal forces leading to the composition of the first English dictionary.

It might be plausibly argued that Robert Cawdrey's *A Tale Alphabetical* (1604), the first English dictionary, would not have been possible if it had not been for this earlier tradition nurtured by the clergy and the schoolmaster. This relationship between the schoolmaster and the lexicographer appears centuries later to have been harmoniously integrated in the person of James Murray. Just as Murray's early training as a schoolmaster was to serve him in good stead later in life during the grinding labors of editing the *Oxford English Dictionary,* so too the teachers and early lexicographers of the Middle Ages and the Renaissance were to unite these two disciplines. The early volumes cited above are chiefly concerned with glossing English and another foreign language, either a classical or a European vernacular. However, the genesis of English lexicography is also indebted to the works of such prominent schoolmaster/grammarians of the late 16th century as William Bullokar, Richard Mulcaster, and Edmund Coote—indeed their influence from the 1580s until Cawdrey's composition of 1604 is critical.

During the 17th century a number of notable lexicographic compositions were published, beginning with Henry Cockeram's *English Dictionarie* of 1623, the first text in English to employ the word "dictionary," and ending with the anonymous etymological lexicon *Gazophylacium Anglicanum* of 1689. Although the 18th century was dominated by the presence of Dr. Johnson's *A Dictionary of the English Language* of 1755, Johnson too was indebted to his predecessors. Nathaniel Bailey's *Universal Etymological Dictionary of the English Language,* first published in 1721, exercised a profound influence on Johnson, and through Johnson on many of the lexicographical endeavors of the 18th and early 19th centuries. Johnson's use of quotations is, however, an important benefaction to the *Oxford*

English Dictionary. Although modern lexicographers are indeed indebted to Dr. Johnson, certain of his positions on language would today be disputed by most linguists. Johnson wanted to, as he said, "ascertain" the language; that is to fix the language against the forces of change. In this respect, despite his genius, Johnson was one with the prevailing sentiments of his age, and in complete harmony with the prescriptive grammarians of the 18th century, notably with Bishop Lowth, whose volume on English grammar had 22 editions during that century. The next major lexicographic achievement was Webster's *An American Dictionary of the English Language* of 1828. All of the above dictionaries from Cawdrey through Webster were intended for general use, and although a number of them are noteworthy, none of them might be called a historical dictionary in the way we use this term when referring to the *Oxford English Dictionary*. The history of English lexicography then has its roots in the Latin Middle Ages, and each stage in the growth of the lexicographer's skill owes something to those practioners who preceded them. Certainly the greatest lexicographer in the English language, Sir James A.H. Murray, was aware of his indebtedness.

Katherine Murray, the granddaughter of James Murray the chief editor of the *New English Dictionary,* or as it was called later, the *Oxford English Dictionary,* has written a thoroughly fascinating and entertaining biography of her grandfather. James Murray was born in the provincial Scottish border village of Denholm. His family lived simply and the young James was forced to abandon formal schooling at fourteen and one-half years of age. Miss Murray tells the interesting vignette of her grandfather as a young boy studying Latin grammar while tending the cattle—although quite inept at cowherding he later became something of a polyglot. Years later in an extraordinary application for a position in the British Museum, Murray indicated that he was able to work in approximately twenty five languages—all of these self-taught. Despite the disadvantage of such little formal schooling—an insecurity that Murray was to wrestle with the rest of his life—he applied himself to all his interests with a passionate enthusiasm. His early interest in languages was not an exclusive one but was simply another facet of his omnivorous appetite for all things that illuminate the past, whether archaeology, geology, or botany—all of which are areas of study in which he developed some considerable skill.

James Murray, although a singular and perhaps an eccentric man, was typical of a certain type of educated Victorian gentlemen. He possessed a profound sense of personal responsibility and had an acute awareness of the preciousness of time. In a New Year's sermon given in 1871 to the boys of Mill Hill School, he states a belief he was to follow throughout his life, "God gave us no time to waste, no moment to pass unhonoured, unimproved," adding that "every man is given a life work to accomplish." This sermon written almost eight years before he embarked on editing the *OED* has almost a prophetic ring to it. Surely his sincere application to this belief was crucial in enabling him to work the, at times spiritually crushing, 80 to 90 hours per week necessary to edit the *OED*. Despite even his buoyant personality and his deeply felt religious convictions the editorial labors at times sapped his strength as is evident in his near physical exhaustion in the spring of 1880.

The story of the life of James Murray after his agreement to edit the *OED* is really the story of the dictionary. Murray, as was his characteristic devotion to work, became utterly absorbed with what he called in the mid-1880s a "never ending toil."

In the course of the biography Miss Murray introduces us to a host of fascinating characters with whom Murray was associated—men like Furnivall, Skeat, Coleridge, Trench, Gibbs, and Jowett. It was Dean Richard Trench of Westminster, Herbert Coleridge, and F.J. Furnivall who, on June 18, 1857, resolved, under the aegis of the recently founded Philological Society, to begin the project of editing a new dictionary of the English language. And it is to Furnivall that we are indebted for the idea of having a host of volunteer readers supplying the subeditors and editors with words and quotations. This material was collected by the Philological Society, and Furnivall in his characteristically ebullient fashion made much of its importance when the Society was negotiating with the delegates of the Clarendon Press. However, James Murray, appointed to edit the "big dictionary" by the delegates, records that on the receipt of the first ton and a half of the *PS* slips from Furnivall, he was dismayed in opening the bundles to see their disarray. He reports that one bundle contained a dead rat, and yet another a thriving family of mice. The portrait of Dr. Furnivall that emerges from this volume is slightly at odds with the sentiments expressed in the Preface to the 1933 *OED,* where we are told that his ". . . genial disposition and constant readiness for new friendships explained his success in enlisting the help of others." This is a minor caveat.

From the Philological Society's meeting of January 1858, it took approximately 70 years to complete the *OED*. James Murray's association with the dictionary began in 1878 and ended on his death in July

of 1915. In those 37 years he was completely one with his massive un-
dertaking. Of the 15,487 pages of the fully edited dictionary, he was
responsible for editing half—a monumental achievement. He was
knighted in 1908 and received the D. Litt. *Honoris Causa* from Oxford University in June 1914. Miss Murray's biography of her distinguished grandfather is well written and a joy to read not only for the
light it throws on her fascinating ancestor, but because it brings into
focus much of the activity of the early pioneers in language study of
the mid and late 19th century in England.

University of Tennessee, Knoxville   Thomas J.A. Heffernan

BOOKS RECEIVED

Charles R. Anderson, *Person, Place, and Thing in Henry James's Novels.* Durham: Duke Univ. Press, 1977. Pp. 308. $12.75.

Thomas M. Curley, *Samuel Johnson and the Age of Travel.* Athens: Univ. of Georgia Press, 1977. Pp. 285, Index. $12.50.

William B. Dillingham, *Melville's Short Fiction, 1853–1856.* Athens: Univ. of Georgia Press, 1977. Pp. 390, Index. $16.50.

Bernard Duffey, *Poetry in America: Expression and Its Values in the Times of Bryant, Whitman, and Pound.* Durham: Duke Univ. Press, 1978. Pp. xiv, 358, Index.

Paul John Eakin, *The New England Girl: Cultural Ideas in Hawthorne, Stowe, Howells and James.* Athens: Univ. of Georgia Press, 1977. Pp. 252, Index. $11.00.

J. Lee Greene, *Time's Unfading Garden.* Baton Rouge: Louisiana State Univ. Press, 1977. Pp. 204, Index. $11.95.

Evans Harrington & Ann J. Abadie, eds. *The South & Faulkner's Yoknapatawpha: The Actual and the Apocryphal.* Univ. of Mississippi Press, 1977. Pp. xii, 212. $3.95.

T. Walter Herbert, *Oberon's Mazéd World.* Baton Rouge: Louisiana State Univ. Press, 1978. Pp. xxv, 200, Index. $10.95.

Jerome Mitchell, *The Walter Scott Operas: An Analysis of Operas Based on the Works of Sir Walter Scott.* Univ. of Alabama Press, 1977. Pp. xiii, 402, Index. $17.50.

Charles Richard Sanders, *Carlyle's Friendships and Other Studies.* Durham: Duke Univ. Press, 1977. Pp. viii, 342, Index. $14.75.

Allen Tate, *The Fathers and Other Fiction,* Introduction by Thomas Daniel Young. Baton Rouge: Louisiana State Univ. Press, 1977. Pp. xxi, 370. $14.95.

Richard Walser, *Thomas Wolfe Undergraduate.* Durham: Duke Univ. Press, 1977. Pp. 166, Index. $8.75.

Floyd C. Watkins, *In Time and Place: Some Origins of American Fiction.* Athens: Univ. of Georgia Press, 1977. Pp. 250, Index. $10.50.

CONTRIBUTORS

MARY ALLEN, Assistant Professor of English at Howard University, has published articles on Melville, Conrad, Hawthorne, and Hemingway, as well as a book, *The Necessary Blankness: Women in Major American Fiction of the Sixties.*

JOHN K. CRABBE, Assistant Professor of English at the Geneseo campus of the State University of New York and co-editor of *English Record,* has published several articles in *English Journal.*

MARC D. GLASSER, Associate Professor of English at Morehead State University (Kentucky), has published essays on film and technical writing and is preparing a study of marriage in medieval hagiography.

KENNETH W. GRAHAM, Assistant Professor of English at the University of Guelph, Ontario, has published numerous articles on Beckford's *Vathek.*

ANTONY H. HARRISON, Assistant Professor of English at North Carolina State University, has published on Swinburne and Ruskin in such journals as *Modern Language Quarterly, Victorian Newsletter,* and *Victorian Poetry.*

JERALD D. JAHN, Assistant Professor of English at Vanderbilt University, has published in *Shakespeare Studies* and has completed a book-length study entitled "Love's Sensual Emperie: A Genre Study of the Elizabethan Minor Epic."

DAVID K. JEFFREY, Associate Professor of English at Auburn University, has published several articles dealing with Smollett and has written on topics in American literature as well.

A.L. and M.K. KISTNER have collaborated on a number of articles which have appeared in *Shakespeare Studies, Studies in Philology,* and *JEGP,* among others. A.L. Kistner is an Associate Professor of English at the University of Colorado, and M.K. Kistner is a self-employed writer.